LOVING MONDAY

Succeeding in Business
Without Selling Your Soul

JOHN D. BECKETT

IVP

InterVarsity Press
Downers Grove, Illinois

Also available from InterVarsity Press:

Loving Monday AudioBook, two 90-minute audio cassettes,
   0-8308-2260-7
Loving Monday RocketEdition, 0-8308-5501-7

InterVarsity Press
P.O. Box 1400, Downers Grove, IL 60515-1426
World Wide Web: www.ivpress.com
E-mail: mail@ivpress.com

Discussion questions ©2001 by John D. Beckett

First edition ©1998 by John D. Beckett

InterVarsity Press® is the book-publishing division of InterVarsity Christian Fellowship/USA®, a student movement active on campus at hundreds of universities, colleges and schools of nursing in the United States of America, and a member movement of the International Fellowship of Evangelical Students. For information out local and regional activities, write Public Relations Dept., InterVarsity Christian Fellowship/USA, 6400 Schroeder Rd., P.O. Box 7895, Madison, WI 53707-7895.

All Scripture quotations, unless otherwise indicated, are taken from the New King James Version. Copyright ©1979, 1980, 1982 by Thomas Nelson, Inc. Used by permission. All rights reserved.

Cover photograph: Michael Banks / Tony Stone Images

ISBN 0-8308-2333-6

Printed in the United States of America ∞

Library of Congress Cataloging-in-Publication Data

Beckett, John D.
   Loving Monday : succeeding in business without selling your soul / Joun D. Beckett.
     p. cm.
   ISBN 0-8308-2333-6 (paper : alk. paper)
   1. Business—Religioius aspects—Christianity. I. Title.
HF5388 .B43 2001
650.1—dc21

                                                                                    2001024406

25 24 23 22 21 20 19 18 17 16 15 14 13 12 11 10 9 8 7 6 5 4 3

22 21 20 19 18 17 16 15 14 13 12 11 10 09 08 07 06 05 04 03 02

"John Beckett takes his faith *and* his work seriously. In this sensitive volume he offers a treasure house of insights into the depths of religious meaning in his own life and its relevance to corporate leadership."
LAURA L. NASH, *Senior Research Fellow, Harvard Business School*

"*Loving Monday* is a wonderful statement of faith and daily life. John has not written from the ivory tower, but draws from experiences we all can relate to in the real world."
CURTIS E. MOLL, *Chairman of the Board, President & CEO, MTD Products, Inc.*

"I heartily recommend *Loving Monday* for managers and business students alike. John Beckett shares his insights and experiences in an easy-to-read format— a practical guide to biblically based leadership in the workplace."
JAMES J. LINDEMANN, Chairman & CEO, *Emerson Motor Company, Emerson Electric Co.*

"*Loving Monday* systematically and skillfully constructs the key principles required for successful business. It is an invaluable tool, reinvigorating me and those I work with."
MARK D. SILJANDER, Ph.D., *Member of Congress (Ret.); Ambassador (Ret.)*

"I'm a pretty calloused reader—especially when it comes to anything in the fields of business management and theology. This book, however, strikes me as extremely fresh and insightful— maybe even inspired. It hit me in both head and heart."
PERRY PASCARELLA, *Author,* *Former Editor-in-Chief,* **Industry Week** *Magazine*

To Wendy

Foreword

Meeting John Beckett many years ago was no coincidence. At the time, I was heading up a major consumer products company in Colorado (you guessed it—the one that bears my family name). My work, along with family, took all my waking hours. I was not aware of any particular lack in my life until Mike, an acquaintance I'd met through a church group, asked me an unexpected question. "How can I pray for you?" he asked.

The words "I need a friend" came tumbling out of my mouth.

I was surprised at my answer. To that point I had never thought about needing a friend. Later, Mike called me to suggest that I meet John Beckett, a businessman from Ohio. "I believe the two of you would hit it off," he said.

Shortly after, John and I arranged to get together for a day of skiing. Mike was right. We did hit it off, and from that point a wonderful friendship began to emerge. We had much in common—especially our desire to be good husbands and fathers—the more so as we learned each of us had six children. But we also discovered a common heartbeat—to run our businesses in an honorable, exemplary way.

A few years after we met, John invited me to speak at his company's fiftieth anniversary celebration. Little did I anticipate what I would find on that first visit to the R. W. Beckett

Corporation. Here was a company tucked away in a beautiful, rural Ohio setting, manufacturing a needed but unglamorous product for home heating. Yet what I encountered in the spirit of their people—their excitement about their work and their zeal for excellence—left a lasting impression. This company, I concluded, was a kind of model—reflecting an extraordinary enthusiasm among its employees, unique approaches to manufacturing, and policies and practices which were not trendy but time-tested, durable and realistic. I saw much that I could learn and even import into our larger and more complex business.

Since meeting John, I've moved on to the leadership of ACX Technologies, a NYSE listed company. John is on our board, so he and I have frequent contact and good opportunities to share ideas, compare notes and encourage one another. Because of our friendship and similar heartbeat for business, we even talked from time to time about coauthoring a book on how to integrate our faith and our work. The press of my business involvements prevented a joint effort from happening. But John kept our mutual vision alive, and as the manuscript for *Loving Monday* took form, I was among the first he called on for review and comment. I knew from reading the first draft that this book would become a significant and unique addition to business literature.

In its few pages, John has captured the essence of what makes a company a principle-based business. He identifies the basis for such an approach, and he gives us hope that we can have great impact on the lives of many people through the realm of our work. *Loving Monday* is not written as a college professor, a theologian or a consultant might write. It is written from the trenches—from one who has experienced firsthand the enormous challenges and rewards that a life in business can bring. It is simple, direct, light-hearted and rich with insight. I kept wanting to turn the pages and discover more that I could apply in my own company. The book reveals the very heart of the man I know so well as my friend and encourager.

I believe you will find, as I have, that *Loving Monday* is a depository of the kind of practical and timely wisdom that will enable you to see your work in fresh ways. I trust it will also inspire you—even as John has inspired me over the years—to find new meaning and fulfillment in your work.

Jeffrey H. Coors
President, Graphic Packaging Corporation

Preface: Coffee & a Bag of Peanuts

Words. Principles. Truth.

Words. Too many words. We're drowning in them.

Principles. They cascade off the shelf of every airport bookstore.

Truth. It's getting harder and harder to find.

But when we do find it, truth is like light from a beacon piercing the fog-laden night—warning us, as the ship's captain is warned, of treacherous shoals, steering us toward safe harbor.

Business is a journey—filled with promise but fraught with challenge. My plan in this book is to help focus the beacon's light on that journey.

We'll move quickly. I know you're a busy person, so my goal is to get you through this book in two ninety-minute plane trips. And that's with coffee and a bag of peanuts.

When my friends learned I was writing this book, they told me to be sure to define my audience.

It took a while, but now I believe I know who you are.

☐ You're in business—or want to be in business some day.

☐ You're a principled person.

☐ You want your company, your profession and the world to be a better place because you've been there.

☐ You're inquisitive, not content to stay as you are.

You'll get to know more about me, but for openers:

☐ I'm in business.

☐ I'm a principled person.

☐ I want to know foundational truths and apply them to the fullest in my work.

☐ I'm eager to share what I've learned, with the understanding that I'm still learning.

Oh—one more thing. You'll see why I really love Mondays.

A final goal. I'll be pleased if this book becomes your friend. If it gives you hope. If it gives you courage. If it gives you fresh vision for aligning your work world with timeless truth.

Acknowledgments

A few acknowledgments are in order. (There could be many more.)

To Wendy, my precious wife, who not only bore our six wonderful children but bore with me in this writing endeavor. (Writers can get really grumpy!)

To Dick Leggatt, a skillful editor whose persistence and encouragement were invaluable.

To our employees, who did just fine without me as I worked on this project.

And to the dog, who got shorter runs in the morning.

Introduction: The Flight Plan

Here is the flight plan for *Loving Monday*.

The book has four major parts: "Foundations," "The Big Picture," "Applications" and "The Wrap-Up."

In Part One, "Foundations," I share some personal experiences—unique challenges that proved pivotal, often revealing vitally important truths. Typically these insights have not come in large doses but in small pieces which, over time, have fit together. Their impact has been profound, shaping my view of life and producing a zeal for business.

In Part Two, "The Big Picture," we take a short philosophical journey to look at Western culture through two distinctly different windows. Viewed through the first, we see work and faith largely detached from each other—two separate worlds. But seen through the second window, work is not worlds apart from faith—the two are remarkably integrated and compatible.

In Part Three, "Applications," we look at specific ways foundational truths can be integrated into every aspect of daily life, especially our work. The distinctive quality of these truths is that they are rooted in the Bible, which I have come to see as an amazing resource with great relevance to business. It is time-tested yet contemporary.

Part Four, "The Wrap-Up," ties the key concepts together and describes their implications for us as individuals in business.

As my friend Jeff Coors says in the foreword, this book is not theoretical but thoroughly rooted in the real world. The backdrop for what you will read is my own experience, including nearly four decades in the work world. But while the stories add flavor, this is not a book about me. Nor is it a "how-to" book: "Just apply these four-step principles, stand back and watch what happens!" Rather, it is a book to anchor us more firmly in some basic principles and open up some different ways of thinking. It is a book to help us see the practical value of applying foundational values in our businesses and occupations.

I'm convinced that truth properly applied produces results. You will find new and fresh ways to bring energy and meaning to what you do day in and day out. Your customers will notice, and your fellow employees will see the difference. You may even prompt an added smile on the face of your accountant!

So, fasten your seat belt. Before you know it, the flight attendant will be coming along the aisle, checking tray tables and seat backs. And you'll be closing this book, ready for your next exciting assignment.

PART ONE

Foundations

1

Peter Jennings's Magnifying Glass

*N*O WAY, I SAID TO MYSELF. *We're not going to let ABC News barge into the R. W. Beckett Corporation, shoot a lot of footage, extract a few sound bites and say whatever they want to say about us on national TV!*

So went my reasoning as I hung up after the phone call from ABC's headquarters in New York. After all, hadn't they told me they were considering other companies they could feature? Why us? It would just be an intrusion, and for what benefit? In fact, the wrong kind of coverage could be damaging.

The news team had learned about the Beckett Corporation a year earlier. I had spearheaded a national effort, taking issue with the Equal Employment Opportunities Commission (EEOC) after the agency had issued a set of guidelines many thought would restrict religious freedom in the workplace—such as the right to display a poster for a religious event or sing Christmas carols at a company dinner. National media had run stories on the resulting controversy. Now ABC News was following up with our company, wanting to learn more of how we were relating our faith to our business practices.

I knew from earlier experiences with the media that we needed to be cautious. I thought back to the time a regional magazine did a satirical feature story on our company, lampooning some of our most important values. On the title page I was piously caricatured in a robe and a halo—not the most endearing way for a CEO to be profiled to the greater Cleveland business community! I didn't want something like that to happen again, especially in front of a national TV audience.

But ABC needed an immediate reply. As reluctant as I was to agree, something that had happened earlier that day gave me pause. In a planning meeting with our senior management team, I had talked about how we could do a better job of making an impact on the marketplace with our core values, such as integrity and excellence. I had referred to a verse from the Bible that speaks about our being salt and light in the world, "a city on a hill [that] cannot be hidden." As I recalled that discussion, I decided it would be hypocritical not to think seriously about ABC's request. We weren't going to scatter much salt or shed much light if we yanked the welcome mat from Peter Jennings, America's most widely watched news anchor.

The day after our affirmative reply, ABC's news team arrived at the company—a camera crew from Chicago, a producer from New York, and Peggy Wehmeyer, a correspondent from Dallas.

The Shoot

"We'll need to be here for two days," said Peggy. "Our crew may do as much as fifteen hours of shooting for our three-minute news segment. We'll need to see the whole operation, talk to your employees, speak with some of your customers and suppliers, as well as people in the community. We want to talk about your policies and practices. We need to interview you."

I could feel the knot tightening in my stomach. "Tell me again what you're looking for," I said, half hoping they would change their minds.

"We understand that you believe your faith has a bearing on the way you do business," replied Peggy. "We'd like to see the evidence of what you're doing. How is it affecting people's lives? How has it made you different from businesses down the street?"

There was no turning back. We were committed to walk out this risky but exciting endeavor—exposing our company, our beliefs and our reputation to ABC's magnifying glass. In spite of my apprehensions, I sensed we were doing the right thing.

"Peggy," I said, "we'll be very open with you—show you whatever you'd like to see and let you speak to anyone you want. But I want to ask a favor. As you know, a lot can happen between now and the final version of this piece. The story can come out a dozen different ways. All I ask for is an honest and fair portrayal of who we are and what we believe."

"John, I'll do my best," replied Peggy. "But the final decisions will rest with Peter. He's my boss and he really runs the show."

Show Time

The night of the broadcast, my wife, Wendy, and I held our breath as Peter Jennings eyed his twelve million invisible viewers:

"We begin another season of 'The American Agenda,' and we start this September with our religion correspondent, Peggy Wehmeyer. It seems to us that everywhere you turn in America these days, millions of people are searching for greater meaning in their lives. Tonight we're going to concentrate on the growing tendency of business leaders in America to have their personal faith make an impact in their companies. In other words, they are using the Bible as a guide to business."

"Whew . . . that's a good start," I said to Wendy, as I eased back slightly on our den sofa.

Peggy's voice came in over the first clip:

Nancy Borer, an assembly line worker, is taking a six-month maternity leave with partial pay. On top of that, her employer made the extraordinary offer of three years off so she can raise her children. Eric Hess assembled oil burners until his employer sent him to school and paid his $1500 tuition. Now he's a plant supervisor.

The man who gave these unusual opportunities to Nancy and Eric is John Beckett, a successful Ohio manufacturer who takes his work and his faith very seriously.

So far so good. But at the next clip, I winced. No, this wasn't home video. It was national TV, and I was looking at my own face on that TV screen.

Instantly I flashed back to Peggy's hour-long interview with me in my office. As a cameraman had threaded the microphone wire down my shirt front, Peggy had chatted about Laura Nash's new book, *Believers in Business,* which she had skimmed on her flight that morning. "The book is great!" she had said. "It identifies seven areas of business conflict which Dr. Nash discovered in her interviews with sixty evangelical business people. These are conflicts between the walk of faith and the practical world of business. An example is the conflict between caring for employees in a downturn versus tending to the bottom line."

I saw it coming: *I'll bet she's going to ask me questions that Dr. Nash took two years to research, and she'll expect sound-bite answers from me.*

And she did exactly that!

One of those questions had concerned my life's purpose. As I sat watching the broadcast, I heard the response to that question that had made it into the final cut: "My main mission in life is to know the will of God and to do it."

I swallowed hard and said to Wendy, "You've just seen a miracle. Of all the jumbled answers I gave in that high-pressured interview, Peggy has extracted my main goal in life in one short sentence."

The rest of the news piece came across wonderfully. The integrity of the company, the enthusiasm of our employees, and the relevance of our core values to the everyday world of work were presented in a clear and compelling manner.

Peggy concluded her commentary by observing that for our company and increasing numbers of business people "lasting rewards cannot be measured in dollars . . . satisfaction comes from building a business without selling their souls."

The unusually positive report hit a responsive chord with viewers, and they let ABC know it. Peggy called me that evening to say the program had prompted the largest number of favorable phone calls ever received for their news broadcast.

We had been put under Peter Jennings's magnifying glass. What he found, although very imperfect, was a manufacturing company in northern Ohio where faith and work were not mutually exclusive but coexisted remarkably well.

What he didn't know as he closed his broadcast that evening was that one very relieved business owner was just then leaning over on the sofa, giving his wife a smooch and saying, "Honey, I think I can sleep tonight."

2

Companions
for Life

*T*HEY ARE USING THE BIBLE as a guide to business." Thus Peter Jennings summarized a small but growing trend in the American workplace. The fact that our company is part of such a trend is gratifying. It might never have happened, however, if my life had taken a different turn at a few key intersections.

I grew up in Elyria, Ohio, a small industrialized town not far from Cleveland. My parents, originally both from Canada, had moved there because my dad had been offered an engineering position with a company in the heating industry. I was born soon after, in 1938. By the mid-forties I had two younger sisters, Beverly and Susan.

Dad and Mother were very principled people who expressed their love, in part, by holding my sisters and me to a high standard. When we stepped out of bounds, they had an uncanny way of finding out. We attended the Episcopal church fairly regularly, but the hour on Sunday was largely detached from the rest of my world.

During my early teens, my parents gave me a handsome black Bible with a leather cover and gold-edged pages. I had been running with a tough group of guys, and I guess they felt it might help.

With good intentions I began reading my new Bible at Genesis, chapter one. (Isn't that how you read a book?) But when I got to the genealogies and detailed rules and regulations given by Moses, I bogged down. Before long I decided this book wasn't relevant to my world of friends, studies, dating and sports. That was it for the Bible for several years.

Wendy
Then, during the summer after my first year of college, I met Wendy. It happened the day I went into the Portage Store—a small grocery outlet for campers and cottagers in Algonquin Park in Canada's north woods. My intent was to buy milk and a newspaper. But I was so dazzled by the beautiful young Canadian gal who waited on me that I left the store in a fog, totally forgetting the newspaper I'd gone in to buy.

Wendy, I discovered, had taken this summer job as a grocery clerk to earn tuition money for entrance into the University of Toronto that fall. It turned out that both our families had cottages on nearby Smoke Lake. On my first visit to see Wendy at her family's cottage, I arrived to find her sunning on the dock, reading the Bible.

Nobody reads the Bible on vacation! I thought. Though I was intrigued with her choice of reading material, that was not the main attraction. I found myself captivated by Wendy's sparkling eyes, her engaging smile and her love for the outdoors. It wasn't long before I realized I'd been smitten and was falling in love. I'm sure my parents were both amazed and amused by my eagerness to do the grocery shopping at the Portage Store the rest of that summer!

In the fall, as I returned to Boston and my second year of engineering at MIT, I found it was especially rough getting back to calculus and physics. Wendy was continually on my mind. I eagerly checked the mail each day, looking for any small clue in her letters that the feelings I had toward her were reciprocal. A visit to her home in Toronto the following Christmas confirmed that she too was falling in love, and from that point on, our relationship became the most important thing in my life.

We were together on every possible occasion over the next four years, especially during the summers. We stayed in touch through a steady exchange of letters, in which we candidly shared our thoughts and feelings (easier by mail than in person, perhaps). The growing prospect of marriage made everything else seem secondary, but we reluctantly concluded it was important for both of us to finish college first.

Working with Max

On my graduation in 1960, I took an engineering position with Lear-Romec, an aerospace firm located in my home town. There, I worked under the leadership of Max Utterback in a department that had responsibility for the design and development of guidance systems for missiles and aircraft.

Max was more than a boss; he was a mentor. He and I conferred by the hour about ways we could use very small electrical forces to position the massive booster engines used to launch spacecraft toward pinpoint targets in outer space. But our talks were more than technical. From Max's experience and wisdom, I gleaned solid insights into the ways integrity and fair dealing had their place in business decisions, large and small. Max had grown up in a home where the Bible was respected and regularly read, and I couldn't help wondering if his strong ethical values and good common sense were in some way a result of the Bible's influence.

Wendy and I were married a few months after her graduation in 1961. For our late summer honeymoon we returned to our much-loved Algonquin Park, this time for a seventy-five-mile canoe trip, paddling across sequestered lakes and traversing rugged portages.

We settled into a modest apartment in Elyria, not far from where I worked. Wendy was hired to teach French in local grade schools. We joined the violin section of a small community orchestra and attended the local Episcopal church. We lived near my parents and were able to see them often. A year after we were married, Kirsten, our first child was born. All in all, we were convinced life could not have been much more perfect. For us, Camelot had come to Ohio—at least for the moment.

That Enigmatic Book Again

During our courtship and early marriage, I noticed that Wendy continued to read her well-worn Bible. But in spite of her example, I simply was not able to get enthused about this enigmatic book. I would try now and then, dusting off the fine volume my parents had given me, but it didn't seem relevant. Again and again I would set it aside. The turning point eventually came in the form of a challenge.

On the invitation of a friend, Wendy and I attended a seminar given by a speaker who based his teaching on biblical principles and their application to everyday life. He offered seminar participants a challenge. "I want to ask you to do something," he said. "I'm asking you to make a commitment—between you and the Lord—to read the Bible every day for at least five minutes."

I like challenges, and I took this one.

At first, reading the Bible daily was sheer discipline. Occasionally I'd crawl into bed and realize, "Oh, nuts! I forgot to do my reading today." On would come the light—out would come the toothpicks to keep my eyelids up. But the dutiful practice continued. Unlike earlier efforts where I began with the Old Testament, I found it more relevant to read the Gospels and Letters in the New Testament. In time, the discipline became a delight. As I began to read the Scriptures first thing in the morning (I changed my routine to a time when I was most alert), it not only saved on toothpicks but helped nourish my mind and spirit throughout the day.

Surprisingly, the much-neglected black Bible from my parents was coming to life. I was amazed to discover how often something I had recently read would apply to a situation I was facing. Almost imperceptibly, I began looking at things differently as ideas and concepts from the Scriptures began shaping my thoughts and attitudes.

Little did I know how timely this new help from the Bible would be, for our little Camelot was about to collapse. Soon we would encounter challenges that would leave us reeling—and would leave me looking for bedrock answers to baffling questions.

3

Trouble in
Camelot

MY FATHER'S INVITATION to join him in his small manufacturing company caught me completely by surprise. It happened one evening when Wendy and I were at my parents' home for dinner.

"John," said my dad matter-of-factly, "Fitz has been my business partner for over twenty-five years. He's going to retire soon. How'd you like to join me in the business?"

I was equally surprised by my response. "Dad, I really haven't thought much about it, but it sounds awfully good to me. Yes, I'd be very glad to join you."

Admittedly, I had some misgivings about leaving the glamour of the high-tech aerospace industry. Probing outer space was at the cutting edge of technology, and it had been exciting to be in the thick of it for over three years. By contrast, I knew the R. W. Beckett Corporation had just a few customers, employed only twelve people, and had barely survived some severe struggles over the years. But the prospect of working together with Dad was irresistible.

My father had begun the business twenty-five years earlier in the basement of his home. In 1937, on the heels of the Great Depression, Dad's only "capital" had been a firm determination to design and build a superior oil burner for residential and commercial heating systems. Shortly afterward World War II broke out, and critical commodities were diverted to the war effort. Burner production halted. To survive, the company went into the home insulation business.

The postwar years were excellent for Dad's oil burner business as homeowners switched in droves from coal to oil heating. In 1951 my father was able to fulfill a lifelong dream—to build his own manufacturing plant in an attractive rural setting just outside Elyria. Soon, however, competition from the natural gas industry severely impacted the business, and for several years Dad was discouraged with the long-term prospects for oil heating. But then, in the late fifties, he shook off the discouragement and, with dogged determination, designed a new, more competitive oil burner. Gradually sales began to pick up. Yet Dad knew when he asked me to join him in late 1963 that it would take his own best efforts—and mine—to rebuild a sturdy business. However, we welcomed the challenge and especially the opportunity to collaborate. I was excited to find myself loving Mondays even more in an oil burner factory than in aerospace!

Collapse of Camelot

Days before I started at Beckett, the nation was stunned by the news that President John F. Kennedy had been assassinated in a motorcade in Dallas. The unthinkable had happened, and overnight people around the globe witnessed a violent end to the notion that we were truly living in Camelot.

Camelot also collapsed for our small family in a succession of blows to our happy and secure life. First, our daughter contracted gastroenteritis, an intestinal illness that leads to severe dehydration. For many infants this condition is fatal. But mercifully, and with some outstanding medical help, Kirsten's life was spared. Soon after, however, Wendy's mother succumbed to a difficult and painful battle with cancer. A lovely and talented woman, Mrs. Hunt had suffered a fall at her summer cottage, causing a back injury which produced a malignant tumor that eventually proved fatal.

Despite the surrounding circumstances, Dad and I were delighted to be working together. I became an eager understudy, learning under his guiding and experienced hand. I envisioned future years in which I would draw all I could from his wisdom and expertise. Perhaps I would succeed him one day—but only when both he and I were ready.

That dream was shattered when I received a phone call on a cold Saturday morning from the local police. Stunned and speechless, I gasped for breath as I received the report that Dad had been found slumped over the steering wheel of his car, the victim of an apparent heart attack. *How can this be?* I thought, my mind in total turmoil. *He was simply driving to work! We were supposed to be working together on that new project in an hour or so . . .*

Dad was sixty-seven, seemingly in good health. He loved his work, and I believe, given the choice, he would have preferred to go as he did—"with his boots on." But for me, at age twenty-six, the news of his death was a staggering reality that I had no idea how to handle.

I later learned from others how much Dad had hoped I would succeed him, though he had never let on. So subtle had he been in that intention that I could have easily missed it and said no to his invitation to work with him. As it turned out, the year Dad and I worked side by side was the most remarkable of my budding career.

During this brief period, my view of him changed from that of stern disciplinarian to mentor and friend. He opened his heart and his expansive mind to me, teaching me in months what could have taken years in another work setting. Ten more years would have found me still in awe of the breadth and depth of his enormous capabilities, but a year together would have to suffice. His death was the most profound reminder yet that the future was uncertain, and that I would need resources well beyond myself to meet the challenges I would most certainly encounter.

I didn't have much in the way of faith to rely on back then. I was just beginning to understand the help the Bible could provide. Beyond that, my only tether to "divine assistance" was through the confidence of Wendy and my mother—a confidence that God was sovereign in all things, including the mystifying loss of my father.

But that wisp of faith, though faint, prompted me to reach out for the sustaining help I needed. I took some faltering steps in offering up prayers—without any clarity at all on whether or how those prayers might be answered. But thankfully there *were* answers.

Encouragement in the Crisis

The first matter I was able to resolve was the unsettling issue of whether to keep the company or sell it. Offers to purchase the Beckett Corporation were coming in from larger companies, and I felt I needed to take them seriously. If I kept the company and it stumbled, all that my parents had worked for, including my mother's financial well-being, could be sacrificed.

Mother took the initiative in putting this concern to rest. "John," she said, "I really am confident you can do it. And even if it doesn't work out, don't worry about me. We have lived with very little before, and we can do it again if we have to." With her stalwart support and a quiet inner sense that keeping the company in the family was the right thing to do, I decided to turn down the offers and do all I could to make the company succeed.

A second critical issue was resolved in an unsolicited assurance I received. The engineering director of our largest customer expressed that company's intent to continue buying oil burners from us. His company could easily have decided to purchase burners from any of several larger and more stable suppliers. Even now, it is hard to fathom what the impact would have been if we had lost this key account, which represented two-thirds of our business. It could well have been the end of the road for the Beckett Corporation.

A further answer to my hesitating but earnest prayers for help came in the form of a person, Bob Cook. Early on, I realized I needed a key executive to help sustain and strengthen the business. Bob amply filled those shoes and soon became our vice president. Together we have forged a tight relationship that has now spanned more than three decades.

I marveled as I realized that in contrast to the bleakness of the loss of Dad, in a matter of weeks we had seen such provision—such specific needs met. *Surely we're out of the woods now,* I remember thinking. *In spite of all that has happened, we can put our full energies into building the business.*

But amazingly, within a few months we were plunged into still another crisis.

4

Trial by Fire

*T*HE PHONE CALL came at 2:00 a.m.

"This is the North Ridgeville Fire Department. Flames are shooting twenty feet above the roof of your factory. We've called volunteers, but they don't know your plant. Is there anything that can explode in there?"

I shook myself. Was this a bad dream? The caller repeated the question, and I realized it was no dream. The company was really ablaze! When I arrived at the plant minutes later, I was stunned. Our warehouse was engulfed in flames. My first decision—almost automatic—was to go in.

The firefighters reluctantly followed me into the eerie, acrid blackness as I pointed to key doorways and areas where volatiles were stored. Flames had now consumed large sections of the metal warehouse and were headed toward the manufacturing area with its wooden roof structure. If that went, with all our machinery and equipment, I knew we were out of business. My worst fears surrounding the decision to keep the company in the family would be realized.

We moved to the front of the building, snaking our way through piles of smoldering cardboard and melted hulks that had been die-cast aluminum oil burner housings. If we could drive the flames back, maybe we could spare the plant and offices. It was our only hope. After two hours that seemed like an eternity, we found we were winning. The main flames were extinguished, the small fires put out.

As the morning sky caught the sun's first rays, the full extent of the damage became clear. It was horrendous. Burned remnants of ceiling insulation hung like black stalactites around the exposed steel beams which, in turn, had been twisted in the intense heat like strands of licorice. Acrylic plastic parts had been miniaturized—shrunk by the heat to a fraction of their former size. Debris, completely unidentifiable, lay in great smoking heaps all over the floor, while a pungent, eye-burning vapor permeated everything.

Singed But Still Standing

How close we had come to a total loss of the company became clear as we surveyed the charred wooden beams of the main plant roof structure. The fire had spread all the way from the warehouse to the plant, yet critical machines, though coated with an ugly brown tar, were operable. Files and important records were intact, even though the foul smoke had left its pungent residue everywhere. With a prodigious effort by employee teams working around the clock and suppliers who rallied to our urgent calls, we were able to fulfill each and every customer commitment on schedule. We needed a miracle, and we received one!

Destiny, I was learning, unfolds this way—in moments, in miracles. In one moment, death. In another, an inferno. But close by, provision—silver linings amidst black clouds. Miracles. Life, when it becomes an unforgiving anvil against which lessons are hammered home, can devastate and dishearten; but that same anvil can also forge character and produce hope.

To me, keeping the business going became more than economic necessity. It was a cause. I didn't realize it at first. But Dad's death, then the fire, convinced me this business *had* to continue. For whatever reason, and whatever the company's destiny, I had been set at the helm. As painful as these experiences had been, they were producing an understanding of larger truths—truths which would be essential in achieving that destiny.

An insight from that same speaker who had originally challenged me to explore the Bible helped me to understand more clearly how God was working in my life:

Vast areas of Scripture will never be meaningful to us unless we go through the experiences for which they give insight. It was for this reason that God allowed all of his servants in Scripture to experience conflicts, and it is for this reason that we go through them as well.

The Other Side of the Mountain
For me, the difficulties I had encountered were only gradually opening up insights into the Bible and into the ways God works

in our lives. But valuable lessons were being forged.

Dad's death, though it seemed so untimely, caused me to develop a dependence on God in ways I never would have otherwise. This upheaval probably accelerated my maturing process by years, helping me to learn to pray and to trust God more completely—not to mention the on-the-job crash courses in finance, marketing, employee relations and plant floor supervision that were essential to keep the company going.

The devastating fire also helped me see that we mustn't become overly secure with temporary things. I realized that factories, machinery, even customers can be here today and gone tomorrow, as can homes, bank accounts and friends. We could install sprinkler systems (and we did!), take out more insurance and exercise normal safeguards. But I was growing in the conviction that God has designed life so we can never be fully secure without him.

During those trying times I found a verse in the book of Proverbs which helped me stay properly focused. Here is what it said: "Trust in the LORD with all your heart, and lean not on your own understanding; in all your ways acknowledge Him, and He shall direct your paths." I realized that as I committed my ways more fully to God, he would watch over me and over that which I held dear.

His amazing care became even more evident in an incident that happened the summer following the fire.

Humpty Dumpty's Greatest Fall

Carolyn, our second child, had been born midpoint between

Dad's death and the fire. She was a year old at the time of the incident. I still tremble a bit as I recall what happened. We were driving north to our summer cottage with Wendy's dad, by then a widower. He had a new car, and we were unfamiliar with the door locks. We all thought the rear doors were locked.

As we sped along the Canadian superhighway, Carolyn was peacefully playing in the back seat (there were no baby carseats yet) with a soft, homemade Humpty Dumpty doll, a pillow stuffed with old nylon stockings. To our horror we turned to see the rear door swing open, ejecting Carolyn to the road beneath.

Providentially, we had just gone onto an unpaved section of the highway that was under repair, forcing us to slow to a crawl. Carolyn hit the packed dirt, clutching her Humpty Dumpty doll, which wonderfully cushioned the blow. Moments later we were lifting her into our arms, her tender body hardly scratched.

Each time we thought about it, we were overwhelmed that on that two-hundred-mile trip, all but a mile or so at high speed, that door flung open when it did! Never had we so dramatically seen such divine protection.

Naturally, we were more careful with locks after that, but more importantly, we saw one more evidence that trusting our ways to the Lord was not just a spiritual exercise but a very practical, sensible thing to do. For reasons beyond what we then understood, he really was helping us on the road of life, working around us in myriad ways we couldn't see.

It was almost as though an Invisible Hand was at work.

5

The
Invisible
Hand

*A*DAM SMITH, WHOSE HISTORIC WORK *The Wealth of Nations* was published in 1776, said there is an "invisible hand" that guides all human economic activity.

Economics alone? Evidence continued to mount for me that this maxim was too limited—that there was an Invisible Hand at work guiding *all* of life. At least the events that had loomed so large early in my marriage and business career seemed to indicate there was a subtle yet profound influence shaping my direction in life—God's Invisible Hand.

This influence had first surfaced toward the end of high school when I began applying to colleges. I saw two possibilities. One was Kenyon College, a liberal arts school in Ohio with an adjunct Episcopalian seminary. By attending there, I reasoned, I could go on to seminary, leaving the door open to some form of ministry. The other option was completely different. It was to apply to MIT, one of the nation's top schools for engineering and science. Acceptance there would point me to a career in business.

Although I felt that ministry would somehow be the "right" thing to do (don't ask me why), my heart was really leaning toward a career in business. My dad had graduated as an electrical engineer from the University of Toronto, and deep down I wanted to be an engineer too. I was anything but certain of the outcome as I dropped the applications into the mail. If college and career were indeed linked, the replies from those two colleges would point me in the direction of my life's work. Anxiously I awaited the responses.

Which Way to Go?

I heard from Kenyon first, with an unqualified acceptance. I was pleased, but not exuberant. Could I possibly be accepted at MIT, my first choice? I knew the competition for admission was as tough as anywhere in the country. A week passed, then a month, six weeks, and still no reply. Then it happened. I was at home the day the mailman delivered the long-awaited envelope with the return address: Massachusetts Institute of Technology, Cambridge, Massachusetts.

Holding my breath, I opened the letter. When my eyes fell on the word "acceptance," I gave a loud and sustained "Whoopee!!!" that echoed through the house, bringing my mother running at full tilt. Never mind that it was conditional on my maintaining at least a C+ average my first semester. I was in. Nothing, I determined, would keep me from becoming a graduate engineer. I was on a career path, at least at this point, toward engineering and the sciences, not ministry. There it was—the Invisible Hand steering me. In any case, I was the happiest senior at Elyria High School on that day in May 1956.

Once at college, however, a measure of spiritual inquiry continued—enough that I attended church regularly and found myself in vigorous religious debates, defending the idea of an omnipotent God. I saw myself as a moral person. I avoided trouble—at least serious trouble.

The Pest

But I was also cautious, especially with the tack taken by a freshman classmate named Dave. Dave kept telling me I needed to be "born again," using terminology alien to my Episcopal upbringing. Regularly, he would "just happen" to be at the intersection where I would start my daily ten-minute walk across the Charles River Bridge connecting Boston, where I lived in the Sigma Chi fraternity house, with Cambridge, where the campus was located. Try as I might, I could avoid neither Dave nor the nettling conversations that ensued whenever he intercepted me.

In a word, what Dave was selling, I wasn't buying. He struck me as narrow, religious and pesky. He seemed to be locked into a formula, and I had an argument to counter every one of his neatly packaged theories.

I heard some of Dave's same formulas presented when, one night during my senior year of college, curiosity took me to an evangelistic crusade meeting. At the conclusion, I strode to the front platform, where a counselor began showing me Bible passages. "Here's the scriptural pattern for changing your life," he said. "Now, John 3:16 says . . . and in Romans 10 . . ." But I still wasn't buying. It seemed too simplistic. It involved faith, and faith didn't seem to square with intellect.

In spite of my unwillingness to accept such an approach, I considered myself an open person spiritually, holding to a certain reverence for God. I even wondered again if I should consider some form of more direct ministry, at least for a period of time. After all, wouldn't that be more worthy than simply plunging into a secular work career?

I've got it! I remember thinking. *I've had two years of ROTC training. I'll do a stint as a chaplain in the Air Force.* That sounded elevated, noble. So I took counsel with Dr. Theodore Ferris, the eloquent rector of Trinity Episcopal Church in Boston where I had been attending most Sundays.

"John," he intoned, "I wouldn't advise going into any kind of ministry unless you truly sense you are called to it. Wait for that call. If it's genuine, you'll know it."

Before long, on-campus interviews began. Boeing in Seattle was the first to offer a position. That was followed by an offer from a much smaller aerospace firm in the town where I had grown up—a company where I had worked as a lab technician the previous summer. By taking a position there, I could not only live with my parents, but I would be a mere three hundred miles from Wendy, still in college at the University of Toronto.

I chose to work with Lear, the smaller firm. Dr. Ferris's wise advice helped me take the business-oriented option with a clear conscience. I simply didn't have the strong sense of call toward ministry, and it would have been wrong to try to manufacture it.

So the slide rule, not Episcopal vestments, became the signature of my trade. The Invisible Hand was at work—shaping, directing the steps of my life.

A Living Reality

In retrospect I realize that during college and the years that followed, I had my spiritual heels unduly dug in, resisting various incremental means by which God was trying to draw me into a deeper relationship with himself. (I'm so grateful he didn't give up on me.) Though much of what I had encountered in the presentation of Christianity during those college years was unappealing, I began seeing in others—especially Wendy and her family—faith that was a living reality. For them, God wasn't aloof. He was personal. They approached him as a close friend.

Wendy's dad was an Anglican minister, in fact the president of a theological seminary. Her mother was an active church leader. But it wasn't their credentials that made the impact. It was the natural way their spiritual views were integrated into the rest of their lives. They seemed to joyfully live and breathe their faith.

Wendy was my greatest example. She "walked out" a quiet yet confident faith—not complex, but sincere, deeply satisfying to her and with winsome appeal to others. So I watched, I admired, and I considered. But I also struggled, time and again thinking, *This faith business defies logic, and I'm not about to put my brain on a shelf. I need to understand more.*

Years passed, encompassing my first job, the beginning of our family and the major challenges of my early years in the family business. My career was firmly launched and successful. I had so much to be thankful for! I couldn't but agree with the evidence that God was involved in many ways in my life and business. Yet here I was, in my late twenties, rigidly steeled against fully yielding to anything I couldn't analyze and reason my way through. *I don't want to become like one of those,* I concluded, recoiling from my image of the stereotypical fundamentalist Christian—blindly accepting, dogmatic, unimaginative and just plain not much fun. How I struggled!

But with the passage of each year, there was a growing sense that I was somehow spiritually incomplete. The Invisible Hand of God was still at work, nudging, prodding, encouraging me to see that there was more.

6

Strangely
Warmed

*J*OHN WESLEY, WHO profoundly impacted eighteenth-century life in America and from whom the Methodist denomination emerged, stated that he felt his heart at one point "strangely warmed" as he placed his full trust in Jesus Christ.

For myself, there came a time in my late twenties when God, in his grace, broke through the doubts I'd had for so many years. It really wasn't my doing, other than a willingness to make room for him. Nor was it based on my getting my act together—getting all scrubbed up so I could be somehow "good enough" to be acceptable. Rather, God himself took the initiative—almost as if he were extending his hand in love to me.

I'm sure there had been other such occasions—times when God had tried to draw me to himself. But finally I accepted his initiative, laying down my fears and reservations. Where I had resisted before, I was now more open to a relationship with him.

In effect, I simply said, "Lord, I trust you, and I want to be fully yours." I thought, *How amazingly patient he has been!*

This must have been what John Wesley meant when he spoke of being strangely warmed. It seems there was a point for him—and now for me—when a very special transaction took place. To my limited understanding it was ill-defined, but to God I believe it was quite specific. I realized I was no longer a casual acquaintance, living in a distant country. In a wonderful way I had become one of his—as though I had become a member of his household, part of a new family. A decades-long process had culminated. A critical piece of a life-sized jigsaw puzzle had been set in place.

It is hard to put into words what I felt at the time, but it was like a struggle that had finally ended. Like the quiet following a thunderstorm. Like a small child, suffering from a fever, who falls off to sleep in its mother's arms, then wakes up well. I relaxed and smiled more easily. People noticed it! There was now an inner joy that went beyond just being happy. It was a sense of wholeness and assurance.

Thinking back, I realized I had judged my college friend Dave, and later the evangelist, unfairly. At the time, the package they had presented was not appealing, requiring a step of faith into the unknown—beyond that which I could see with my eyes or fully understand with my mind.

But they possessed and offered me a kernel of priceless truth: that the way into a full relationship with God comes through a type of death—giving up our hold on our own lives and our old way of living—and then rebirth, accepting a new life offered to us by Jesus Christ. I concluded this was what they meant by that strange phrase *born again*. It was not a physical thing but a spiritual one.

Whose Business?

My everyday life was different now. Initially I didn't give much thought to the implications this pivotal step toward God would have for my work. I was, frankly, caught up in all that was taking place in me spiritually.

In time, however, practical questions began crossing my mind, not unlike questions that had occurred earlier. *Is my involvement in business truly my calling, or is it more a matter of personal preference? Should I be thinking about some more direct form of ministry?* I wanted to have these important issues resolved, and so I determined to make them a matter of prayer.

Answers weren't immediate. But after several months, and to my surprise, I sensed it was I who was being asked a very key question: Would I be willing to completely release my involvement in the company and follow a very different direction in life?

Wow! I really didn't want to hear that question. I put forth my best arguments for staying put—continuing the family heritage, providing for my mother and for the family, applying my technical and business expertise. But I concluded this wasn't a negotiating session. Instead, God was probing deep into my heart, examining my motives.

After a good deal of soul-searching, I responded to the query by making perhaps the most difficult decision I'd ever made—a decision to release to God my future and all that I owned, including the company. In essence I said, "This business can't be mine and yours at the same time. I don't want to hold onto this or anything else unless you want me to. If you are asking me to forego this vocation and do something different, I'm willing— willing to trust you for the company's future and mine, whatever that may be."

What occurred as a result of that decision was a watershed.

Somehow it seemed God needed to know I was prepared to fully yield everything in my life, including my work, to him. The wonderful irony is that in return came the unmistakable assurance that I *was* where I belonged—in business. It was as if God were saying to me, "John, I needed to know you were willing to follow me, whatever, wherever. But you are where I want you to be. I have called you to business."

I couldn't recall a time when I'd had a greater sense of his affirmation and peace.

The Faith Connection

This experience, my releasing everything to God and then, in effect, his placing it back in my care, brought me into a whole new dimension of understanding of and commitment to my work. I was not out on a limb by myself, hoping I was doing the right thing. Instead, I had a greater sense of correctness and purpose than ever before—that I should, in fact, be doing just what I was doing. Gone were the doubts that I was missing God's highest for my life!

And yet, a troublesome issue emerged: How should I relate my faith to my work? As I looked about, I saw very little evidence that people of faith were carrying their faith into their work. Their two worlds were disconnected. To be honest, I had to admit I was no different. Sundays were Sundays, with the rest of the week largely detached, operating by a different set of rules. *Can these two worlds that seem so separate ever merge?* I wondered. Little did I realize what a key question that was, and how much the answer has been mangled in modern society.

7

Two Worlds,
or One?

As MUCH AS MY CONVERSION had begun a process of transformation in my mind and spirit, I realized there was a wide gulf in my thinking between this new dimension of faith and how it applied to my work. True, I saw that certain Scriptures could bring guidance or comfort to work-related situations. But by and large I found myself in two separate worlds. Significant growth was taking place in both—but largely unrelated.

During that time, in the late sixties, some basic business decisions had set the stage for sustained expansion. In fact, the Beckett Corporation grew each year—and kept growing—at a compound growth rate exceeding 20 percent for most of the next two decades. Key decisions helped fuel that growth—hiring talented personnel in sales and engineering, refocusing our marketing efforts on major oil companies, forming a network of distributors and dealers, developing a new generation of fuel-saving burner units, and enlarging and improving our plant facilities and equipment.

We borrowed heavily to fund our growth, and we were fortunate to generate sufficient cash flow to repay our debt ahead of schedule. We were a small fish in a large pond, but we gained growing recognition for our technology, good customer service and support. Ours was a youthful and aggressive team, willing to take risks. In time the rewards became evident.

The Home Front

My business activities were exhilarating but bore little direct relationship to what was happening away from work. Our third child and first son, Kevin, was born in 1967, just as I was entering a new dimension in my walk with the Lord. A few years later our third daughter, Catherine, was born. Wendy and I were thoroughly devoted to our four precious children, but nothing exceeded my desire to grow spiritually during this dynamic period. I suppose I was a little like a plant that had just sprouted, and for a season one new shoot after another sprang forth.

Wendy and I attended and even helped sponsor numerous Christian teaching seminars, helping solidify and accelerate the growth of our faith. We met in small "cell groups" in homes for fellowship. We discovered a growing number of good books about Christians who were making a difference. Seeing the great interest among our friends in such literature prompted me to link up with several other businessmen to establish a Christian bookstore, which for years served the greater Cleveland area with biblically based books and audio and video teaching materials.

Increasingly, I found the Bible had become my primary spiritual life-source. The decision to read it each day was bearing good fruit, bringing a gradual renewal in my thinking. But I still hadn't made the connection that its great insights related directly to my work and could be instrumental in shaping our company's policies and practices.

Nor did I see that the Lord himself, with whom I was becoming increasingly better acquainted, would actually guide my thoughts and actions in very practical business matters, if I would allow him to do so. It wasn't long, however, until a situation developed in the company that shook me to the core, forcing me to turn to the Lord in a more direct way.

The Wake-Up Call

I had grown up with the understanding, largely from my dad, that companies and their employees were better off in a union-free environment. But I also knew we could do only so much to influence such decisions—employees under the law were free to form or affiliate with a labor organization whenever they chose. As I thought about such a possibility in our company, my reaction was always one of raw fear. One day, that which I feared came upon us.

When I received the news that an organization attempt was underway, that fear became almost paralyzing in its intensity. Then the fear turned to anger—anger that some of our employees would consider such a course, rather than talking with our management about their concerns. Soon the anger turned to the sober realization that we had to act, wisely but decisively, if we were to have any hope of staying union-free.

The Campaign

I sought out a local labor attorney, known in our town for his tough approach to organization attempts. He agreed to help us. Then, just a few weeks into the development of our campaign, he suddenly died of a heart attack.

The pressure of this situation, if nothing else, prompted me to earnest prayer. Faced with our attorney's death, I almost concluded we should handle the situation by ourselves, rather than starting all over with an unknown lawyer. That was until I happened to be reading from the book of Proverbs and, to my surprise, my eyes fell on a very pointed verse. In the translation I was reading at the time, Proverbs 12:15 said, "Don't act without the advice of counsel!"

Well, within a few days we had located an attorney from Cleveland who, as it turned out, gave us outstanding advice, helping guide our month-long campaign to rebuild our employees' confidence in the company.

As I thought through what was at stake in this organization attempt, it became clear to me that the most important thing we could lose was our direct relationship with our employees. I genuinely cared for our people, then numbering nearly thirty on our plant floor. I knew there was no way an outside organization, permanently interposed between employer and employee, could bring the same dimension of care and concern. Rather, in all likelihood, it would actually obstruct what should be a close working relationship.

This, too, I saw as a biblically based position, directly addressed in the sixth chapter of the apostle Paul's letter to the church in Ephesus. There, employers are reminded that the way they conduct themselves with their employees should be a reflection of the caring and compassionate way each of us is treated by our heavenly Father.

So with conviction, good counsel and a sound strategy, we shared our views and concerns with our employees, all within the tight guidelines imposed by the National Labor Relations Board. A vote was taken, and the overwhelming decision of our employees was to stay union-free.

Making Adjustments

We were greatly relieved and thankful. We believed God had helped us, guiding us through this difficult time. But it was also a tremendous wake-up call. I realized we had neglected communication. Many aspects of our employee policies and practices were not well understood. Some of our benefits were substandard, and we promptly took steps to improve them. We developed a new employee handbook, made some changes in supervision, and took much more seriously the growing mandate I was now convinced we had—to work more closely together with our employees, clearly communicating our goals and aspirations and seeking the best possible work environment for every person in the company as we moved forward.

As a result of this gut-wrenching experience, I also began to realize that I could not, or should not, be living in two separate worlds. For over a decade, I had seen clear evidence that the Lord had a vital interest in my work. I concluded it would be utterly foolish for me to somehow partition my life into one way of thinking and conduct on Sundays and another during the work week. There needed to be a much fuller integration of my two worlds.

This seemed to me to be a practical and sensible way of looking at faith—that it encompassed the full spectrum of life. But there were still gaps in my understanding. Later I more fully realized there are cultural reasons why it is so difficult for us, especially in the West, to see our work and our faith as unified—to see them as parts of one world, not separated into two.

This is the focus of the next section of the book. The insights discussed there have totally transformed my thinking—and the thinking of others with whom I have shared them over the years.

PART TWO

The Big Picture

8

Culture
Wars

A<small>S I ENTERED A NEW DIMENSION</small> of spiritual understanding in the late 1960s, I began to realize how dramatically the culture in our nation was changing. By comparison, there was an innocence to the decade of the fifties, the years when I attended high school and college. Certainly there were problems, but such basic concepts as right and wrong, truth and falsehood, honor and dishonor, were better understood and accepted. They seemed to be woven into the fabric of society.

In the sixties these values were ripped from the social fabric. Our civility was jolted by the assassinations of President Kennedy and Martin Luther King, the removal of prayer from schools, the Vietnam war, Woodstock, and radical unrest on college campuses. The turbulence of this period uncoupled much of our society from an already declining acceptance of traditional values, creating a legacy that today forcefully impacts the world of business. Nowhere has this been more evident than in the university classroom, as Charles Colson discovered in a visit to Harvard a few years ago.

As a guest speaker in an ethics course at the Harvard Business School, Colson, who was involved with the Watergate scandal and is now head of Prison Fellowship, addressed the abandonment of traditional and biblically based values. As he recounts in one of his books, he told the students that Harvard could never teach business ethics because the school did not believe in absolute values—the best it could do would be to teach pragmatic business judgments.

"You can't teach ethics here because you don't believe there are moral laws," he said. "But there are moral laws just as certain as there are physical laws. We are simply unwilling to admit it because it interferes with our desire to do whatever we please, and doing what we please has become the supreme virtue of our society. Places like Harvard, indeed Harvard of all institutions, propagate these kinds of values."

Colson's speech was met by passive silence, then polite applause. Anticipating a more hostile reaction, he later queried organizers of the event: "Why such a docile response?"

"The material you presented was totally new to them," said one young man. "They didn't have the tools to debate it" (Jack Eckerd and Charles Colson, *Why America Doesn't Work*).

Unchanging Truths

Absolute values. Moral laws. Such terminology presupposes a basis, a standard by which truth and falsehood are measured. Not so many years ago, the response to Colson's remarks would have been different. The sobering reality is that what business school students are now being taught is rooted not in unchanging truths but in moral relativism and situational ethics, depriving them of the kind of solid foundation they will need in their work. In contrast, as recently as in the 1920s, business publications like the *Harvard Business Review* regularly made reference to well-anchored truths transmitted through our nation's Judeo-Christian heritage.

As much as institutions like Harvard have strayed from our nation's historical cultural roots, the problem actually goes back much further. Discerning the tap root that still nourishes modern Western culture will help us understand more fully what is happening, not only in our elite business schools but in many of our modern businesses in the West. And it will help us gauge our own attitudes toward our work and callings.

To take on this somewhat philosophical topic, I will need to depart briefly from the narrative of my experiences in business. If you're like me, delving into philosophy requires some "heavy lifting." But I believe you will find it very worthwhile. For me, it has been nothing short of revolutionary to discover that a system of thought going back over three millennia has so affected the society in which we live and work today.

One more note of encouragement as you wade into the balance of this short section. Gaining clarity on this topic will also provide a good foundation for moving into Part Three of this book, "Applications." There I will relate landmark lessons we've learned, drawing from our efforts to integrate a culturally different, biblically based perspective into our day-to-day work. I trust you will readily see how it all fits together.

So keep your seat belt fastened. If you encounter some turbulence, it won't last. Before you know it, we'll be on our final approach for landing.

9

A Greek Legacy

A FEW YEARS AFTER my conversion, when the spiritual side of my life took on new depth and meaning, I began to discover how uniquely the Bible applies to the day-to-day. But I also discovered how alien a biblical view was to much of what I had come to accept through my education and experiences.

In Western culture, the lens through which we view the world has been colored by nearly three thousand years of Greek thought. You know the names. Homer. Thales. Socrates. Plato. Aristotle. What they thought and taught has had a profound impact on how we think.

From these Greek thinkers came much that is good, including mathematics, the scientific method, the beautiful language of the New Testament, and the Hippocratic Oath, which medical practitioners have followed verbatim until the last few decades.

But our inheritance from the Greeks also came with some

serious baggage. The Greek thinkers, shunning the God of the Hebrews, came up with man-centered and mystical notions to define the world around them.

Some have been largely discarded, like Homer's gods of fire and thunder, living on mountain peaks. Four hundred years after Homer, and four hundred years before Christ, Aristotle departed from mythology to describe "God" as an infinite but impersonal "energizing form," a self-developing energy source—the very root of modern New Age philosophy.

Without the God of the Bible, human beings are left with only themselves. Protagoras, in the fifth century B.C., put it crisply when he offered his famous maxim, "Man is the measure of all things."

Such ideas, even when wrong, don't die easily. Much of what we see in society extols Greek thought—whether it's the opening ceremonies of the Olympic games, news periodicals, radio and TV programs, movies, business seminars or educational curricula at our colleges and public high schools. Adoration for the Greek system is everywhere.

Absolute or Relative?
Moral relativism, for example, didn't start at Harvard or other universities. Socrates, using his famous "dialectic method," had his students arrive at their own ideas of the meanings of such things as goodness and justice. They formed personal notions of right and wrong. Thus, they justified living within their own opinions. Socrates couldn't teach absolutes he hadn't embraced. Nor can we.

Greek thinking affects our culture in other ways, and it has had a significant impact on the way we feel about business in general and our work in particular. To understand the impact we must follow the logical progression.

The Greeks couldn't get away from the concept of "dualism"—the idea of higher and lower planes of ideas and activities. Plato was the clearest on this. He sought to identify unchanging universal truths, placing them in the higher of two distinct realms. This upper level he called "form," consisting of eternal ideas. The lower level he called "matter." This lower realm was temporal and physical. Plato's primary interest lay in the higher form. He deemed it superior to the temporary and imperfect world of matter.

The rub comes when we see where Plato placed work and occupations. Where, indeed? In the lower realm.

Dualism in the Christian Era

Nearly a thousand years later, in the fifth century A.D., Augustine sought to merge Platonic thought into a Christian framework. This approach resulted in a distinction between "contemplative life" and "active life"—the same distinction between higher and lower, but with different names. The higher of these realms came to be equated with church-related concerns that were considered sacred, such as Bible study, preaching and evangelism. Other things were secular, common, lacking in nobility.

Where did Augustine place work and occupations? As with Plato before him, in the lower realm.

Thomas Aquinas, in the thirteenth century, furthered this

derogatory notion of work as he perpetuated the dualism of Greek thinking. He also categorized life into two realms, which he called Grace and Nature. Revelation, which gave understanding to theology and church matters, operated in the upper realm of Grace. In the lower realm of Nature, man's "natural" intellect stood squarely on its own.

Business and occupations, operating in the lower realm, didn't require revelation. According to Aquinas, they survived quite well on a diet of human intellect and reasoned judgment.

Lower or Higher?

Now we bring this dichotomy up to the present.

Francis Schaeffer, one of the modern era's greatest thinkers, wrote on the more recent impact of dualistic thinking. In *A Christian Manifesto,* he speaks of the flawed view of Christianity advanced through the Pietist movement in the seventeenth century.

Pietism began as a healthy protest against formalism and a too abstract Christianity. But it had a deficient, 'platonic' spirituality. It was platonic in the sense that Pietism made a sharp division between the 'spiritual' and the 'material' world—giving little, or no, importance to the 'material' world. The totality of human existence was not afforded a proper place. Christianity and spirituality were shut up to a small, isolated part of life.

The result of such a view is that the activity of work is removed from the sacred realm and placed squarely in the secular—making it "impossible" to serve God by being a man or woman in business. To me, this is a startling revelation!

Now here's a question for you. Has this view affected you, as it has me?

Second-Class?

I can now see that the perspective of the Greeks, established so many years ago, continues alive and well to the present day, influencing and distorting our perception of work. For years, I thought my involvement in business was a second-class endeavor—necessary to put bread on the table, but somehow less noble than more sacred pursuits like being a minister or a missionary. The clear impression was that to truly serve God, one must leave business and go into "full-time Christian service." Over the years, I have met countless other business people who feel the same way.

The reason is clear: Our culture is thoroughly saturated with dualism. In this view, business and most occupations are relegated to the lower, the worldly, the material realm. As such they are perceived to lack dignity, spirituality, intrinsic worth, and the nobility of purpose they deserve.

Schaeffer, looking back over the legacy of nearly three millennia of Greek thought, proposes this radically different view of true spirituality:

It is not only that true spirituality covers all of life, but it covers all parts of the spectrum of life equally. In this sense there is nothing concerning reality that is not spiritual.

Indeed, there is a dramatically different way to view the world and our work—a view that liberated me to see business as a high calling.

But to find this view, I had to look through a different window.

10

A Different
Window

*T*HE JEWISH TALMUD tells a story of an elderly rabbi's counsel to his young nephew. The boy already knew the Torah, the Old Testament Law. Now he wanted to study the wisdom of the Greeks.

The rabbi recalled God's words to Joshua: "You shall meditate on it [biblical law] day and night."

"Go, then," said the rabbi. "Find a time that is neither day nor night, and learn then Greek wisdom."

Like that rabbi, who put little stock in the value of studying Greek philosophy, Tertullian, an early Christian theologian, wrestled with the conflict in his day between Greek and Hebrew thought. He asked: "What has Athens to do with Jerusalem?" (Christian Overman, *Assumptions That Affect Our Lives*).

What was so different? Basically, the sources were different. The Hebrews depended primarily on revelation, inspired directly by God. The Greeks, who didn't acknowledge the one true God, depended on humanly inspired reason.

Because the sources were different, the results were different. Different views of deity, of origins, of absolutes, of truth resulted in different worldviews.

Common Principles

Abraham Kuyper, a dynamic Christian thinker who became prime minister of the Netherlands in the early 1900s, addressed the students of Princeton Theological Seminary in 1898. He said this concerning worldview:

> As truly as every plant has a root, so does a principle hide under every manifestation of life. These principles are interconnected and have their common root in a fundamental principle; and from the latter is developed logically and systematically the whole complex of ruling ideas and conceptions that go to make up our life and worldview. (Abraham Kuyper, *Christianity: A Total World and Life System*)

A. W. Tozer, in *The Pursuit of God*, describes the result of the shift in views this way:

> One of the greatest hindrances to the Christian's internal peace is the common habit of dividing our lives into two areas—the sacred and the secular. But this state of affairs is wholly unnecessary. We have gotten ourselves on the horns of a dilemma, but the dilemma is not real. It is a creature of misunderstanding. The sacred-secular antithesis has no foundation in the New Testament.

Biblical thought is not dualistic. There is no "higher" and

"lower." The psalmist said, "The earth is the LORD's, and all its fullness." True, in the Old Testament there were distinctions between sacred and secular, but even these temporary distinctions were abolished in New Testament Christianity.

How we view our work, then, is profoundly influenced by the worldview we choose—the Greek model or the biblical (Judeo-Christian) model.

The Unified Life

Larry Peabody focuses on this issue in *Secular Work Is Full-Time Service,* the most helpful book on a biblical view of our work I have ever read:

> In the New Testament God does not depict the Christian life as divided into sacred and secular parts. Rather, he shows it as a unified life, one of wholeness, in which we may single-mindedly serve him, even in our everyday work. The glorious, liberating truth is that in Christ, God has performed the impossible. In Christ, that which was once secular has become sacred. The wall between them has been removed. 'For everything created by God is good, and nothing is to be rejected, if it is received with gratitude: for it is sanctified by means of the word of God and prayer' (1 Timothy 4:4-5).

Christian Overman depicts the contrast between Greek thought and biblical thought with two diagrams in his excellent book *Assumptions That Affect Our Lives.* I'm grateful for his permission to reproduce them here.

Figure 1 illustrates what we covered in the previous chapter, the widely held dichotomy between two realms—the higher, which is sacred, and the lower, which is secular. This is the worldview of the Greeks:

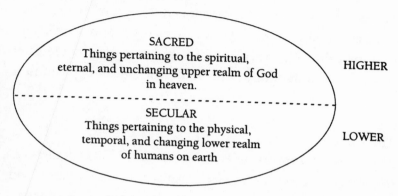

SACRED
Things pertaining to the spiritual, eternal, and unchanging upper realm of God in heaven.

HIGHER

SECULAR
Things pertaining to the physical, temporal, and changing lower realm of humans on earth

LOWER

Figure 1. Greek Worldview (Dualism)

As noted previously, in the Greek view businesses and occupations inevitably end up in the lower realm.

In contrast, the worldview depicted by the Bible holds that all things are good when in harmony with God's design, or evil when in conflict.

In conflict with God's design ("evil") ⇐

church
school
art
home
music
drama
sports
business
law
labor
agriculture
sex
medicine

⇒ In harmony with God's design ("good")

Figure 2. Biblical Worldview

In figure 2 is a list of various vocations and activities, but without regard to rank or worthiness. The distinctions between secular and sacred, higher and lower, don't exist. Overman says God's intent is that "every aspect of human existence and each divinely sanctioned institution is equally obligated to function in harmony with God's will, not in opposition to it."

The Deciding Factor

Any of these endeavors can be in harmony with God's design—or in conflict. Take art, for example. Choices made by the artist will determine whether a painting or sculpture draws the observer toward that which is noble and good or toward that which is base, ignoble and evil. Our homes, our work, medicine, sports—even sex—can be in harmony with God's will or contrary to it. So the deciding factor is not a matter of higher or lower, or sacred or secular, but whether it is in harmony with God's will.

When I saw this distinction—this contrast in worldviews—I wanted to do cartwheels. If I hadn't grown up as a proper Episcopalian, I probably would have! I realized how much my thinking had been negatively affected by Greek dualism.

In stark contrast to my prior thinking, the Bible enabled me to view my work as having great worth to God, provided I would bring it into harmony with him in every way possible. As a believer and a business person, I was no longer a second-class citizen. Nor did I need to leave my Christian convictions and biblical values outside the office entrance when I headed into work on Monday mornings.

A biblical worldview has awesome implications for those of us in the secular, Greek-thinking West. As we allow it, the Bible speaks to us concerning government, economics, education, science, art, communications and, yes, business. Really, it speaks to all of life.

11

Enduring
Truth

As I took more seriously my own study of the Bible, I began to see how detached business had become from the truths that have served us well for so many years. From the earliest days of our nation, and against long-standing Greek influence, a biblical norm emerged to form the bedrock of our ideas and values. We have our Pilgrim forbears and their followers to thank for imbedding such solid thinking into the prevailing culture of America.

But as well as those sturdy (and successful) ideas have served us, with frightening speed they have lost favor, the landscape instead dotted once again with "contemporary" humanistically based alternatives. In retrospect, Greek thought was never really that far beneath the surface.

Do you recall days in the not-too-distant past when, instead of lengthy and convoluted legal contracts, a simple handshake was sufficient? Do you remember when it was rare to lock the door of your home or give a second thought to walking the streets of your neighborhood after dark?

Unfortunately, a mammoth shift in our culture has muscled out character qualities that were the trademark of our nation. This is graphically illustrated in the widely popular work of Stephen Covey, one of America's most respected authors and lecturers to business people.

A Radical Shift

In his #1 national bestseller, *The Seven Habits of Highly Effective People*, Covey quantifies what I have witnessed in my own involvement in business—a radical departure from our nation's historic values. He undertook an in-depth study of success literature published in the United States since 1776 and found a startling pattern emerging in the content of the literature:

The success literature of the past fifty years was superficial . . . filled with . . . techniques and quick fixes . . . with social Band-Aids and aspirin. . . . In stark contrast, almost all the literature in the first 150 years or so focused on what could be called the Character Ethic as the foundation of success—things like integrity, humility, fidelity, temperance, courage, justice, patience, industry, simplicity, modesty and the Golden Rule.

Thus, in little over a generation, we have largely abandoned the enduring character qualities that shaped our history.

With myself, lessons learned while growing up left indelible impressions—for example, when my parents returned to a store where they'd made a purchase to give back extra change made in error by a clerk. Or the day my dad and I were transporting a wheelbarrow in the trunk of our car and were unaware it had slipped out onto the highway. We went back to look for it and discovered it by the roadside, being watched over by a good-hearted man who had seen it fall and stayed to be sure we would get it back safe and sound. Or the wonderful example of Max, my first boss and mentor, who was incensed by every form of dishonest conduct, from padded expense accounts to building excess charges into government contracts. The "everybody's doing it" mentality didn't cut much slack with either my parents or Max.

The Biblical Root

As I studied the Bible in greater depth, I saw its strong emphasis on both absolutes and character. Its moral boundaries were unambiguous. For example, three of the character qualities mentioned by Covey—integrity, humility and justice—are dominant themes in the Scriptures. In just two books of the Bible, Psalms and Proverbs, the word integrity is referred to nine times, humility eleven times and justice a remarkable twenty-nine times.

I discovered that the book of Proverbs taken by itself is a veritable gold mine of practical wisdom and insight. As a speaker at a recent business leaders' luncheon succinctly put it: "Do you want to know how to run your business? Get a Bible and read the book of Proverbs."

Over the years, I have come to a firm conviction: It is of incalculable worth to us that we have at our fingertips the wonderful eternal truths of the Word of God. Even the Bible itself testifies to its own value and validity. "The entirety of Your word is truth," says the writer of the 119th psalm. And speaking of its permanence, he says: "Forever, O LORD, Your word is settled in heaven."

Roasting the Kill

The Bible, I have found, is much more than a theoretical standard. It is a reliable and practical life-directing compass. For example, it may surprise you to learn that a passage from chapter 12 of the book of Proverbs had something to do with my decision to write this book. It says, "The lazy man does not roast what he took in hunting." Obviously this proverb doesn't say anything about writing books! However, as I looked into the background, I discovered the verse speaks of a hunter who kills a large animal in the woods but doesn't do the hard work of bringing it out, skinning it, butchering it and providing it as food for others.

I thought, *I'm not like that man—I work hard, and I'm anything but lazy.* Then I felt the Lord's nudge—reminding me I've had a lifetime of rich experiences in business in which he has shown me many things that may help others. For me to not write about it would be laziness. It would be like not roasting what I took in hunting. The result of that impression from Proverbs is the book you now hold in your hands—an example out of my experience that the Bible can help provide practical direction for the decisions we make.

So the Bible is an incredible resource to us, a sturdy and reliable guide. It has become for me a kind of corporate compass. The more I spend time with it, the more I am instructed, challenged and encouraged by timeless truths that reach into every area of my life—including day-to-day aspects of my work.

Life's Classroom

And it is to this realm that we now turn in Part Three. To the practical, where "the rubber hits the road." To the kinds of issues we face in the world of work, where we need wisdom and insight to know and to do what is right. The Beckett Corporation, with all of its flaws, will be our frame of reference, for it has been our "laboratory"—a place where we have learned much, often stumbling, but then picking ourselves up again.

In addition to telling of our experiences, I will endeavor to link the lessons we've learned on the plant floor and in the office to insights from the Bible. Ultimately, this is the deposit I want to make through this book, for long after each of us has come and gone, the Word of God will remain. Its truths are for all seasons and for all generations.

I also want to emphasize that the specifics of what we have learned in our business may or may not apply to your situation. Just as you as an individual are unique, every enterprise is unique, with a "corporate personality" crafted by its people, history, products, services, practices and even problems. When it comes to applying the lessons learned from someone else's experience, the advice a friend of mine offered as we were eating a fish dinner is helpful: "It's important to eat the meat and spit out the bones." If something I share does not ring true for you and your situation, feel free to simply discard it.

But I have confidence that you will find, as we have found, these two basic realities: first, there are vital aspects of your faith that can be transported into your work; and, second, the Bible can serve as a dependable and unfailing guide in making that connection.

May what we've learned—and are still learning—help you, even if only in a small way.

PART THREE

Applications

12

Infinite Worth

WE LEFT THE NARRATIVE at the end of the first section of this book in the mid-seventies. Back then, the Beckett Corporation was small but gaining momentum. I trust you kept your seat belt fastened during the turbulence of Part Two, "The Big Picture," and came through without too many bumps or bruises. In a moment, I want to fast-forward to the mid-nineties, picking up on the visit by Peggy Wehmeyer and the ABC News team to our company. But first, a quick recap of the twenty years in between.

During those two decades, our business experienced enormous changes. Our sales multiplied over twelve times, and our employment quadrupled. We saw our industry consolidate, with fewer remaining competitors. We encountered a variety of new challenges that tested us severely, including two huge international energy crises. Nonetheless, by the mid-eighties our company had emerged as the world's largest producer of oil burners for residential heating. In addition, we were able to diversify successfully by starting two significant new businesses in related product areas, such that at this writing, the combined companies employ well over 500 people and generate about $100 million in annual sales.

We've chosen to stay private, and we are now seeing the next generation of family members come into positions of leadership, including Kevin, our eldest son, and Morrison Carter, our son-in-law, married to Kirsten, our eldest daughter. On the home front, two sons, Jonathan and Joel, had been born by the mid-seventies, increasing our family to six children, three sons and three daughters. More recently, we've had the special blessing of grandchildren added to the family.

What Makes You Different?
By the time Peggy arrived to do her story in the summer of 1995, it was obvious she had done her homework. She was aware that the R. W. Beckett Corporation had become a market leader in the heating industry. She knew that the company had achieved a fine reputation in the community and that we were sought after as a place to work. But as a reporter on a mission, she was interested in news—especially the type that would support her inquiry into the relationship of our faith to our work.

She promptly got down to business, probing, digging, wanting to know what made the Beckett Corporation distinctive.

"John, how is your business different as a result of trying to apply biblical principles?"

I knew that what set us apart went beyond the fundamental

success factors that characterize many other fine businesses—good products, high quality, careful attention to customer service. It was a different quality, one that is often missing in today's workplaces.

"Peggy," I said, "it's probably in how we regard our people."

"Can you be more specific?" she replied. "Every business I know talks about the importance of people, but there are a lot of employees out there who have really been burned. They feel their companies care about everything else more than them. I hear it all the time—the bottom line, shareholder value, return on investment . . ."

"I know," I said. "I see it firsthand. I personally interview final candidates for every job in the company, and I hear some very sad stories of how people have been mistreated in previous jobs."

"You interview them all? That's pretty unusual. Why do you do that?"

"I began doing it many years ago when I realized how much it built understanding and trust with a new employee. Of course, they're usually pretty nervous, having to meet the boss. But I try to put them at ease. I get them talking about themselves, their interests and hobbies, what they've done and what they'd like to do. It's amazing how valuable those fifteen or twenty minutes are. After all, it's the beginning of a relationship that may last for decades."

"I can see the value," said Peggy, "but is there a biblical principle involved here?"

Gatekeepers
"I noticed in the Old Testament that ancient walled cities had

gates, and elders would sit by them, determining who came in and went out. I saw a parallel. Those who come through our 'gates' as employees will have a profound impact on the success of our company. I try to assess character issues like a willingness to work, respect for authority, basic temperament. Will this person fit in well with our other employees? Basically, is he or she right for us? I even try to meet the spouses of candidates for senior-level positions, helping them understand our company."

"And the track record?" asked Peggy.

"Certainly we make mistakes," I said. "But I believe the thoroughness has resulted in an exceptional workforce. Many have made the company their career, and we find a consistently high level of morale and pride. A good indication is how positively they speak about their work with friends in the community."

Individual Worth

"I'm not sure we've touched on the key issue yet, John. Just *why* the emphasis on individual worth?"

"I think the important thing is to view people the way God does. We see that view initially in Genesis, the very first book of the Bible. There, in describing creation, it says God formed men and women in his own image and likeness. That's really quite remarkable. Attributes unique to human beings—the capacity to think, reason, worship, understand joy and sorrow, use language—all spring from God's own nature.

"When I saw this, it really changed the way I viewed not only myself but other people. I concluded I must place a high value on each person and never look down on another, regardless of their station or situation in life. Peggy, there's something sacred about every individual. Since God attributes unique and infinite worth to the individual, each one deserves our profound respect."

Peggy continued her questioning. "Is this view expressed in any of your statements of corporate philosophy?"

"Yes, it is," I said. "We have established three 'Enduring Values' which are to be embraced and applied throughout our companies. One of these is *profound respect for the individual*. We say that we want our work and work relationships to be dignified, challenging, rewarding and enjoyable. We make the well-being and continuous individual growth of our employees high priorities."

Capturing the Concept on Camera

"John, I'd like to keep talking," Peggy said, "but we've got a camera crew ready to start shooting. We need to see some visible evidence of how things are different at your company."

I had to stop and think. How might our emphasis on individual worth best be portrayed? After all, policies and practices, by their nature, become ingrained in a company—part of the culture, often unseen.

As we talked about the company's distinctives, Peggy picked up on our policy for parents of newborns. I explained that in studying this topic, our management team learned that the first three years of a child's life are critical in establishing a close bond between mother and child—a bond that can produce lifelong benefits. Once the mother is away for more than twenty hours a week or so, that bond is noticeably weakened.

As a result, we established a policy giving employees the choice to stay home up to twenty-six weeks. During this period we maintain their income at one-quarter the normal level and will loan them an additional one-quarter, providing a total of up to half of their normal wages. Then they can return to work part-time, sharing their job with another or doing work at home (both depending on availability), for up to three years after the birth of their child.

Peggy got excited about capturing this benefit on video and set out with the film crew to the home of Nancy Borer. On their front porch, Nancy and her husband (over the objections of their infant in arms) explained how much it meant to them that Nancy could be at home with their child.

The camera crew then visited another home where Chuck and Patty Visocky proudly presented the children they had recently adopted from Colombia, South America—four orphans from the same family. To help in the adoption, the company provided paid time off for the Visockys to travel to Colombia. We currently have a policy of providing parents $1000 for each adopted child. I explained to Peggy that in a day when the value of children seems to be diminishing, we want to take a different direction, emphasizing their value.

The ABC team then delved into our educational policies, talking with several employees who were taking courses to advance their skills. They chose Eric Hess for their interview. Eric's father had worked at the company as our director of quality. When Eric graduated from high school, his dad recommended that he apply. Eric began on the plant floor and showed very good work habits and attitudes. In time, an opportunity opened for him to become a lab technician. But after several months in that position, he concluded it was not right for him.

Some companies consider it the end of the road for an employee when a promotion is turned down, but we encouraged Eric to return to a job in the plant similar to the one he'd left. He simply hadn't found his niche yet—and that process would take some time. Later, Eric expressed interest in supervision. He was tested, confirming his aptitude for leading others. He entered an educational program for supervisors, paid for by the company, and in a short time he became one of our most able people in that key role.

Profound Respect
So Nancy, Chuck, Eric and others told their "sound bite" stories, each capturing a dimension too often missing from the workplace—genuine care and regard for the individual.

In a masterful way, Peggy and the camera crew portrayed our view of the value of the person, and ABC's viewers were able to see another side to business—a human side, one based on dignity and intrinsic worth. As I pointed out to Peggy, the human side and the economic side aren't mutually exclusive. "We've also been able to produce above-average profits and excellent returns to the shareholders," I said.

I'm convinced most employees want to see their companies prosper. They know their success depends on their employer's success, and they will work hard to contribute. But they must be provided a dignified and supportive work environment. They must be viewed as valued, important, worthy. They bear God's own image. If they are of infinite worth in his eyes, they certainly deserve no less from us than our profound respect.

13

Blueprints

A BLUEPRINT ACCURATELY and thoroughly describes all that is needed to complete the plan of the designer.

Sometimes it is easier for us to see God as the Great Designer of the universe than to see him as the Meticulous Architect of our lives and destiny. But whether for a galaxy, a planet, an organization or an individual man or woman, the Scriptures indicate there is a direction determined by God. It is purposeful, not random. It is ordered, not disordered. Some are called in one way, others in another way. Some are gifted or equipped in a particular manner, others differently. One will be given a certain sphere of activity; another will operate in a very different sphere.

Understanding God's blueprint helps us understand more fully our opportunities and responsibilities in the workplace.

I realize this as I think about Jerry . . .

Jerry started with our company right out of high school,

working on the plant floor. Like his peers, he expected to do this work for a short while, then go on to something else. But he found that he enjoyed the work relationships and even found the work itself both interesting and challenging.

He was a good athlete and played shortstop on the company's softball team, helping spark the team to a winning season in a city league. There, rubbing shoulders with employees in other companies, he realized things were pretty good where he worked, and he started thinking about a longer-term involvement.

One day, he caught a line drive right to his heart. Jerry got the eye of Belinda, an attractive young secretary who had joined our company in a product acquisition we'd made. They were soon married, and Belinda left her work to care for their family. Money was tight, but by careful management they were able to get by on Jerry's income, with a little help from secretarial odd jobs Belinda could do out of their home.

Jerry got more serious about his career and took some courses at the local community college. Soon a position opened up for a lab technician in our engineering department. Jerry applied and was the successful candidate. He learned the technical details of our products and was a particular help in bridging the gap between engineering and the plant floor, because he knew the production processes and people so well.

Moving Ahead
The company was increasing its field training, requiring us to work closely with installers and contractors. An opening occurred for a trainer, and Jerry was again the successful candidate.

He got out with our customers and made a fine impression with both his technical knowledge and his people skills, reinforced by a strong moral character. (Customers still call to tell me what a great job he does and how positively he speaks of the company.) When he wasn't out teaching, he helped staff our toll-free "hot line," providing help to service people calling with technical questions.

The company decided to install a fitness center, and Jerry volunteered some spare time to help with the process. Later, he became the head of an employee team to oversee the center's activities and promote the overall concept of fitness among our employees.

Recently, he was appointed to the top position in our training program, with several others working for him. He is so highly thought of that Jerry was voted that year by our company's senior management to receive the President's Choice Award, presented at our company's Christmas dinner.

The Unique Plan

Jerry is a treasured employee. We have every expectation that he will continue to advance, growing in the ways he contributes, and enjoying it in the process. He has a destiny in God. There is a plan that is unique for him. He was created for a purpose. I feel we are at our highest and best as his employer if we can provide a context for his growth and enable him to find and fit in with God's blueprint for his life.

There are many others like Jerry in the company. Penny, for example, began with us as a temporary clerk over twenty years ago. Today she is our director of human resources and a member of our senior management team. Penny's contributions have been tremendous over this period, her competency and value growing steadily.

I am so gratified to be surrounded by folks like this, who genuinely love Monday.

Earlier I mentioned three dimensions of God's plan: *calling*, *gifting* and *sphere*. Here they are in more detail.

Calling

We usually think of a *calling* in religious terms—such as a calling to the ministry. But a calling to a vocation goes beyond just the religious connotation. We can be called to the arts, to athletics, to government service or to business. If it is God's call, it is a legitimate and high calling. In other words, you can be an "ordained" plumber! People called to business have many opportunities for service unavailable to those who are specifically focused on ministry vocations.

We tend to overlook the call to nonreligious vocations that many prominent biblical figures had at various times in their lives. Joseph was an administrator to Egypt's Pharaoh, Moses and David tended sheep, Peter was a fisherman, Lydia managed a garment business, and Paul made tents.

One of my favorite examples is Daniel, a young man taken captive by the Babylonians. He was a person of sterling character and exceptional ability, called to be the equivalent of today's civil servant (in a foreign post not of his choosing!). So compelling were his wisdom and conduct that King Nebuchadnezzar promoted him to ruler over the whole province of Babylon and to chief administrator over all its wise men. Later, Daniel's effectiveness caused him to rise to key positions under other heathen kings.

Leaders in business can be instrumental in helping people find and fulfill their calling.

Michael Novak, a Roman Catholic theologian, covers this important point well in *Business as a Calling*. He quotes Kenneth Lay, chairman and CEO of Enron Corp., the largest natural gas company in the U.S.:

> I was, and am, a strong believer that one of the most satisfying things in life is to create a highly moral and ethical environment in which every individual is allowed and encouraged to realize their God-given potential.*

At our company, we take care in the interview process to discern

---

*In mid-2002 InterVarsity Press, the publisher of *Loving Monday*, contacted me concerning the above reference to Ken Lay. "Do you want to keep this in? With the collapse of Enron, Lay isn't exactly the best example of the point you're making!"

Initially I agreed to find a substitute. Then I recalled the candor of Scripture—the unvarnished accounts of esteemed leaders who stumbled. I view Ken Lay in this light. In fact, six months after the collapse, in an April 26, 2002, interview with *The Wall Street Journal*, Lay restated his commitment to the people in his company: "One of our great successes at Enron was creating a culture, an environment, where people could try to achieve their God-given potential. . . . I was always on the forefront of trying to make sure that our people did in fact live and honor [our] values—respect, integrity, excellence. Integrity and character are incredibly important to me."

Yet the article also tells of how in 1999 Enron relaxed conflict-of-interest rules that were designed to protect the company from the very kinds of transactions that brought it down.

A call to lead involves great responsibilities. Good intentions must be backed up with unrelenting vigilance. Leaders must walk the talk, and must take care that others they seek to lead do so as well.

whether the applicant is being called to work with us. We find it helpful to have multiple interviews and then compare notes. We conduct a series of tests, looking for a match-up of skills with our needs in the workplace. We check references to learn from past work experiences. We commit our hiring activities to prayer.

It makes a tremendous difference later on, especially when an employee is struggling with something at work, when he or she can say, "I know this is what I'm called to do. I am supposed to be here."

Gifting

The Bible also speaks about how various people are *gifted* or *equipped*. In the apostle Paul's first letter to the Corinthians, he speaks of how different gifts complement each other, using the analogy of the human body: "For in fact the body is not one member but many. . . . But now God has set the members, each one of them, in the body just as He pleased."

We especially see the application of this principle of gifting in the placement of people. Jerry is a good example of a person with latent skills that needed to be developed and given opportunity. Eric, mentioned earlier, hit a blind alley before his gifts were identified and he moved into supervision, where he has excelled.

More and more we place an emphasis on people working in teams, where a blend of giftings is particularly important. One may be more analytical; another has greater verbal abilities. One works best with details; another is good at seeing the big picture.

Performance evaluations are a valuable tool in counseling employees. In using them, we obviously look back in review of a person's performance, but the main emphasis is looking forward: What do you want to prepare for? How can we help?

Cross-training is also a helpful guide. A person is placed in another assignment on a temporary basis: for example, a production employee works in inventory or quality control. After this new work experience, the person will have a much better idea of whether to prepare for a different type of work in the company and possibly take courses toward that goal.

Sphere

The third dimension of God's blueprint is *sphere*. In the book of Acts we read that God "has made . . . every nation . . . to dwell on all the face of the earth, and has determined their preappointed times and the boundaries of their dwellings." You live in a certain period of history and were born in a certain place by God's design. Likewise, God sets us into areas of responsibility. The apostle Paul was conscious of this when he told the Corinthians he was determined to operate within the limits of the sphere God had allotted him.

Our businesses have spheres which involve areas of expertise—core competencies. Whenever we go very far outside these areas, we can get into trouble—a fact borne out by the recent unwinding of many conglomerates whose management naively thought that if they could do one thing well, they could do everything well. We do best when we stay with the things we know. Even the brilliant basketball player Michael Jordan learned this lesson when, for a season, he donned a baseball uniform!

To me, it is a great comfort to know that we don't have to be good at everything. It's a relief to be able to say no with a clear conscience when we realize that a request is beyond our area of call or outside our sphere. This is simply the recognition that there is a blueprint for us in God's design.

I've observed over the years that God's grace is most available when we're operating in our areas of calling, gifting and sphere. When we step outside those areas, prompting an inordinate struggle to get things done or to be effective, it may be time for a reality check. We may be seeing an indication that we have pushed beyond the boundaries of God's grace and are expecting more than he is pleased to give. This can be true for individuals and for businesses.

In contrast, it is a wonderful thing when we are centered in our calling, utilizing our giftings, operating in our God-appointed sphere.

As much as possible, we want our workplace to provide such an environment. As with Jerry, our employees are people of destiny. They need to be in a work context where nurturing, experimentation and growth are encouraged, where God's high calling can be realized—where they can discover and fulfill his blueprint for their lives.

14

Trouble, Trouble, Toil & Trouble

*I*N SPITE OF THE BEST BLUEPRINTS, things don't always work the way they were intended to. It seems we cannot run from trouble or avoid difficulties.

We spend a lot of time planning and taking preventive measures to avoid trouble, as indeed we should. Despite our best plans, however, trouble finds us. There is a reason for trouble, for pressure, for difficulties, for the hassles of life. The uncomfortable truth is they are part of God's design. But when we encounter them, they can leave us frustrated, confused and discouraged. It's true in families, and it's true in business.

As a teenager, I had an encounter with trouble that helped me understand how difficulties should and should not be handled. The lesson has served me well throughout my work career.

Trouble Finds Us
I had just turned thirteen, and I was enjoying a short but very

special vacation with my dad at my uncle's summer cottage in Canada's north woods, six hundred miles from home. There, trouble found us when an incident between Dad and my uncle, his older brother Harold, erupted into such a heated dispute that our brief vacation was about to come to an abrupt and bitter end.

It began innocently enough. Uncle Harold got the notion that his young nephew might like to look over his favorite playing cards which featured—you guessed it—a gallery of well-endowed naked women. As I was gawking at pose after enticing pose, Dad walked into the room, eager to get out on the lake to fish for large-mouth bass.

Maybe it was my furtive glance and clumsy effort to hide the cards I was holding—or maybe it was the uncanny instinct a father has when his kid is at risk. Quickly taking in the situation, Dad exploded: "Harold, how could you do a lousy thing like this?"

Harold was stunned. "Reg, get off your high horse. He's a young man. You can't shield him forever!"

"Pictures of pulchritude" were part of Harold's world. He was an artist, the highly esteemed architect who had designed some of Canada's most stunning homes, office buildings and public gardens. To him the nude was art, something of great beauty. Not so, countered Dad. This was raw pornography. And here was his own brother, nearly sixty—not some misguided youngster—callously exposing his son, John, to a tawdry and shameful display.

"Pack your bags, John," Dad fumed. "We're going home."

A few minutes later we crawled into our small cedar boat. With a single pull, Dad started the outboard motor and we pulled away from the dock. I bit into my lip, attempting to mask my intense disappointment. Why did this have to happen? Why did this very special outing with Dad have to abort in a rage of tempers and harsh words?

Making Things Right

A hundred yards from the shore I turned from the distant horizon to glance back at Dad. Normally he would be letting me run the boat. But this morning he was in charge, though I was sure I saw tears moistening his tanned face. Suddenly, with a determined yank on the tiller handle, he said grimly, "John, we're going back." I was sure he'd forgotten something important.

In the distance, I could see Uncle Harold standing at the cottage window, staring out at the lake. As the boat drew nearer, he began trudging down to the dock to find out what had gone wrong. Then I saw something else. In those brief moments, Dad's intense, righteous anger had met with an equally powerful and deep love for his brother. The former was giving way to the latter. Dad was coming back to make things right. Too many years. Too many shared experiences. Too much was at stake to allow this incident to become a festering wound, one that might never heal. Better to make amends now.

My head still swirling, I watched in amazement as these two forceful, strong-willed brothers met on the dock and reached out at the same moment into a prolonged embrace. Few words were spoken. Few were needed. They understood. Never again would Harold violate Reg's fatherly care for his son. Never again would he underestimate Dad's intense sense of right and wrong or risk such a breach.

We unloaded the boat and were now able to complete our vacation—the air wonderfully cleared and the seeds of a vital life lesson deeply sown.

Dad's passion for his beliefs had caused him to risk fracture with the eldest of his five brothers. Yet, without compromising that passion, he had found a place for forgiveness and reconciliation. By God's grace, he faced the problem and conquered it, not the other way around. And in the process, he left an indelible lesson with his son—that we cannot turn our back on trouble. Perhaps his example helped provide the endurance I would need years later when faced with seemingly insurmountable difficulties in my business and in other areas of my life.

Trouble—Even in the Bible
The Bible is remarkably candid, describing the difficulties, temptations and trials men and women have faced throughout history. Not one of those whose lives are portrayed in the Scriptures avoided problems.

The Genesis account of the first human beings makes it clear that the difficulties we encounter were not God's original intent. He created Adam and Eve in an ideal situation where they enjoyed intimate fellowship with their Creator. When Adam and Eve sinned through disobedience, this relationship was permanently altered. All creation, including the human family, came under a curse characterized by toil and trouble.

Jesus came to begin the restoration of all that was lost by Adam and Eve—a process that will one day be complete. The book of Revelation peers into the future: "And God shall wipe away every tear from their eyes; there shall be no more death, nor sorrow, nor crying. There shall be no more pain, for the former things have passed away."

But that day has not yet come. Nor can we, through our best efforts, achieve heaven on earth. Jesus was emphatic on this point as he spoke to his disciples: "In the world you will have tribulation; but be of good cheer, I have overcome the world." The word in this passage translated *tribulation*, or *trouble*, is used elsewhere to describe crushing grapes or olives in a press!

God, in seeking to redeem all that could be redeemed, began using this same trouble for his purposes and our good. James pointed the early church toward a redemptive view of struggles when he wrote, "Count it all joy when you fall into various trials, knowing that the testing of your faith produces patience."

I, for one, am not inclined to count trouble as joy. I fuss, I worry, I try to work through problems with my own brute force. But I am gradually coming to see that God is right there in the midst of the problem, wanting to show us the way through difficulties—not around them—and in the process to teach us more about his ways.

Trouble Finds Us at Work

There has been no shortage of trials in my own business career, and I'm sure the same is true for you. Incidents mentioned earlier—including my dad's sudden death, the devastating plant fire and the union organization attempt—stretched my natural capacities to the limit and mercifully took me beyond, into a deeper walk of faith. Over the years, we've encountered major industrial accidents, employee problems, product liability issues and financial pressures.

As we look back, we can see how each of the problems has had a redemptive value. We can chart our company's maturity and stamina not by what happened on the mountaintops, but by the lessons we learned in the valleys.

Such was the case when the Arab States embargoed oil in 1979, with the resulting run-up in the price of all petroleum-based products, including the heating oil used by our residential and commercial burner customers. To some degree, everyone was affected. You may recall the long lines at service stations during this period when gasoline could only be purchased on alternate days.

That crisis had a frightening impact on our business. Who needs an oil burner if there's no oil? Most of our major customers severely curtailed purchases, and some stopped buying altogether. We were especially vulnerable because we had just completed a large expansion of our facilities. One of our major competitors became so discouraged that they pulled back most of their product development and even their selling efforts. To them, there seemed to be no way out.

A Positive Response

In our efforts to see the large picture, and after consultation and prayer, I concluded we should take a different tack. Instead of retreating, we would become more aggressive. We not only stepped up new product development, but we sent some of our management team out on the speaking circuit, encouraging our customers to see beyond the immediate problem and even take advantage of it by replacing older, inefficient heating systems with modern, fuel-saving units. The idea took hold. We sold hundreds of thousands of replacement units, enabling us to hold our production levels and keep our entire workforce active through the dark days of the crisis. We actually emerged from this traumatic time even stronger, becoming the leader in our industry—a position we've been able to maintain ever since.

Though we have often had difficulty seeing God's purposes in the midst of the problems we've faced over the years, hindsight has revealed his prevailing design and intentions. Over and over, we have seen the truth of what the prophet Isaiah said, that God's ways are not our ways, but are infinitely higher.

Difficulty is God's instrument. Its lessons can be embraced or shunned, but eventually they must be learned. In God's economy, there seems to be no other way.

15

The
Compassionate
Enterprise

*O*UR RESPONSE TO TROUBLE when it visits can leave us in one of two places. Either it will harden us, making us bitter, even vengeful, or it will make us softer, more forgiving and understanding.

I believe God's intent is the latter—to bring us to a place of greater compassion. Over time, compassion will become a distinguishing attribute of an organization—not at the expense of accountability or effectiveness, but as the mark of a business that cares about people and highly regards their intrinsic worth and potential.

A Surprising Call

As I noted earlier, I was on the receiving end of a compassionate enterprise when I suddenly had to take the reins of the company after my father's death. Our business was in a precarious position with sales of just over $1 million, spread unevenly among a handful of customers. Most of our eggs were in one basket—a company in St. Louis that made furnaces for mobile homes. Dad had a good relationship with them, but I had just come on board, and this customer hardly knew me. Faced with my father's passing, they would have had every justification for finding another supplier.

The call from their engineering director caught me by surprise.

"John," said Bernie, "I want to say how sorry we were to hear about your dad's passing. We grew very close, and I looked at him almost as my own father."

I swallowed hard, knowing that as much as they appreciated Dad, they had a tough decision to make. I doubted we could sustain the loss of their business, but this was not the place to say so.

Bernie continued: "I know you must be concerned about our future burner purchases. I want to assure you of our complete confidence in you. We will continue buying your products. There won't be any change from our standpoint."

I could hardly believe my ears. As the words sank in, it was as though a thousand-pound weight lifted from my shoulders.

"Bernie," I replied, "I don't know what to say. I know you don't have to do this. There are several companies that would love to have your business. But I'll tell you this. We will move heaven and earth to be a good supplier to you. We won't let you down."

Bernie's response reflected compassion that is often absent in the modern business setting. His company was taking a risk, and Bernie knew it. But he also knew we were accountable to meet their needs. One major slip on our part and compassion would likely have been out the window. As it turned out, we rose to the trust placed in us, and we have now been their sole supplier of burners for over three decades.

Parallel Truths

The experience with Bernie's company is a good example of a principle which has application in the workplace: truths in the Scriptures often run on parallel tracks.

Two ideas may seem to be in opposition to each other—until they are fully understood when viewed together. The parallel truths in the bold step taken by Bernie were *compassion* and *accountability*. These two complement each other. Neither on its own is complete. Compassion without accountability produces sentimentalism. Accountability without compassion is harsh and heartless. Compassion teamed up with accountability is a powerful force—one which we have found can provide a great incentive to excel.

In business, it is not enough that compassion and accountability simply be present. They must be in balance. The modern work world is characterized by imbalance, with the scales heavily tipped away from compassion toward accountability. A way to begin bringing them into balance is found in the Golden Rule, which requires us to put ourselves in the shoes of the other person.

The model for biblical compassion is found in Jesus Christ, where we see great sensitivity toward the person but also a commensurate requirement for responsible action. A good example is the story in chapter 8 of the apostle John's Gospel about a woman who was brought to Jesus, having been caught in the act of adultery. The Jewish law for this sin required death by stoning—a cruel, protracted form of execution.

Her accusers saw this as a chance to test Jesus. But in response to their charges against the woman, Jesus merely bent down and "doodled" on the sandy ground with his finger. When they continued pressing him, he looked up and said, "He who is without sin among you, let him throw a stone at her first." One by one the accusers left, convicted by their consciences.

Then Jesus addressed the woman, asking if anyone condemned her. "No one, Lord," she responded. "Neither do I," he said. "Go and sin no more."

In his admonition that she sin no more, we see accountability balancing the Lord's clear compassion. So it was each time Jesus extended mercy. There was an expectation that the person would take responsibility.

Compassion at Work

In our work, we find opportunities all around us to show compassion. Here are some examples:

☐ A person is passed over for a promotion for which he or she has applied. We find it is good to meet with such persons, show appreciation for their stepping forward, point out how they can strengthen their qualifications, and encourage them to apply for a future advancement.

☐ An employee has suffered personal loss, a death or serious illness. It is a time to show compassion—face to face where that is possible. Our eyes and our demeanor show that we care. Would we not be grateful for such compassion if we had experienced the loss?

☐ A customer has a reversal and needs an extension of credit. Of course we must be mindful of the risk, but our understanding and extra help, if possible, can bring lasting loyalty and good will.

☐ Perhaps the most difficult of all is the termination, the most dreaded job a manager faces. I find it important to separate the two critical steps involved. First, I go through whatever process is necessary to make a firm decision. This is the analytical step, dealing squarely with reality. The second is the termination itself, which should be carried out with all the compassion I can muster. An effort should be made to cushion the transition, such as a severance arrangement and possibly the use of outplacement services. But a key is to see the process as redemptive, a step which the Lord can use to accomplish his larger purposes—in the person's life and in the organization.

Advent Industries

Some years ago, during a time of high unemployment in our area, we found an unusual way to extend compassion in the workplace. In our hiring, we were getting the best of the job candidates, but I was sobered by the large numbers who needed work and yet were virtually unemployable. With records tarnished by crime, substance abuse or dropping out of school early, they would be the last to find work.

We decided to do something about it. I spoke with Ed Seabold, a business acquaintance, about the concept of starting a new company to hire and train these disadvantaged people. Ed, a no-nonsense manager with a heart of gold, immediately offered to leave his current work and run it. Advent Industries was born, set up as a profit-making company to do subcontract work for our company and other area businesses. When we went to the schools, the police and the courts to find people "bad" enough to fit our employee profile, they were more than cooperative in providing us "worthy" candidates.

Soon, Advent was employing over fifty people in a demanding but supportive work environment. For most of these employees it was their first legitimate job. We had to teach them how to work, how to respect authority, even how to cash a paycheck.

We knew how far we had to go the day Ed left his office door locked while he was out for a few hours. On his return, he unlocked the door and noticed that someone had been inside and had made coffee. Querying the workers, he learned that a few of them had simply removed ceiling tiles, dropped down through the ceiling, made their coffee and gone back to work! That was the last time Ed locked his office.

Compassion combined with accountability has brought great reward during the twenty years Advent has been in business. Over a thousand people have gone through its program, which lasts six months to two years. Many washed out, unable to handle the disciplined work environment. But many others have gone on to success in other area businesses. As a result of their experience at Advent, they possess not only the needed skills, but also a sense of self-worth and purpose.

Every business enterprise has the opportunity to be "The

Compassionate Enterprise." Biblical truth, custom-tailored for each situation, makes the way possible. The powerful example modeled by Bernie years earlier has permanently cemented for us the truth that compassion, not just accountability, belongs in the workplace.

16

Extraordinary Service

*H*AVE YOU EVER BEEN on the receiving end of extraordinary service? If you have, you're almost certainly a repeat customer. And you've found a business that is just about guaranteed to do well.

An incident involving Jim, our general sales manager, describes such service. The fact that I didn't hear about it until months later made it all the more special. Even then, it came up casually, in connection with something unrelated.

Jim had learned that one of our smaller customers had placed insufficient orders and was out of a particular part. Even though it was over the Christmas holidays, they had hoped to run their factory. But without the parts from us, they would have to shut down. Unknown to anyone but his wife, and unheralded within our company, Jim drove a hundred miles one way through a snowstorm, the parts in the back of his car, to keep the customer in operation. Needless to say, Jim's unselfish initiative cemented an already good customer relationship.

The idea of serving is firmly rooted in the Scriptures, particularly in New Testament Christianity. Those cultures which have been most impacted by the gospel generally have a strong underlying ethic of service. Conversely, in many cultures the idea of serving a customer doesn't even exist. The closest term to *customer* in the Russian language is *user of production!*

The Model Servant

Jesus is our unexcelled example of true servanthood. In his own words he makes it clear that he came to serve, not to be served. The apostle Paul cites this aspect of the Lord's character and encourages us to have a similar outlook. One paraphrase of Paul's letter to the Philippians is especially descriptive:

> Let Christ Jesus be your example as to what your attitude should be. For he, who had always been God by nature, did not cling to his prerogatives as God's equal, but stripped himself of all privilege by consenting to be a slave by nature and being born as mortal man. And, having become man, he humbled himself by living a life of utter obedience, even to the extent of dying, and the death he died was the death of a common criminal.

Here we see the true nature of servanthood. The Lord came to earth in complete humility, even though he is the Author and Sustainer of all creation. His servant nature was evident beginning at his birth, which took place in a rude feeding trough for animals. He lived modestly, holding virtually nothing in his possession, but he gave to others lavishly and continuously.

Jesus made himself so available to others that he often had to stay up through the night to get time to pray. He resisted every attempt by his fellow Jews to promote him to the role of a ruling monarch. At the end, he was falsely accused, made an open spectacle, sentenced unjustly under intense pressure from an unruly mob—and he died on a cross, a crude and shameful form of execution.

In all that Jesus did he was a model. His impeccable example was embraced and lived out by his early followers, who understood the joy in sacrifice and the reward in serving. Theirs was not a life of comfort or convenience, but they turned the world upside down through extending themselves on behalf of others. Nor did it stop there. Throughout history, Christ's life has reproduced in his followers the fruit of extraordinary sacrifice, extensive volunteerism and immeasurable benefit to others, on a scale no other religion or philosophy can demonstrate.

The Serving Organization

How realistic is it to expect to apply the concept of biblically based service in today's often harsh, always demanding business environment? In our company, a starting point has been to make our expectations clear, as expressed in our Corporate Roadmap, a printed statement of our core beliefs and values that we use to provide direction for our entire workforce:

> We commit to being very attentive to our customers, going beyond servicing them to satisfying their highest expectations. We pledge to be responsive, following through on commitments while avoiding any kind of arrogance or indifference.

We desire to be predictable, reliable and trustworthy, willing to go the extra mile for something we believe in.

We don't have to look far for ways in which to follow through. The tone in which phones are answered, how we handle the irritated customer, how aggressive we are in remedying problems, all knit together to define our service character or its lack. Jan Carlson, former CEO of SAS Airlines, describes these encounters as "moments of truth"—occasions, if we choose, for extraordinary service.

Here are some of the specific ways we've sought to bring a higher level of service to others:

☐ We expect our internal as well as our external customers to be well served. An "internal customer" is anyone who receives services from another, such as a manager who receives a letter typed by a secretary, or an employee who receives a performance review from the boss, or a person in final assembly who receives a part from the welding or paint department. Each such transaction—and they are occurring between people in business all the time—provides a prime opportunity to serve one another.

☐ We find we must keep our external customers visible throughout the organization. Occasionally our production employees visit customers' plant facilities. There they can meet their plant-floor counterparts and ask them directly about ways to improve what we do for them.

☐ Uncompromising quality goes hand in hand with service. We have put sophisticated quality systems in place to help assure that we are delivering substance, not hype.

☐ An Employee-of-the-Month is nominated and selected by

fellow employees, based in part on unselfish cooperation with others. The employee is recognized by a professionally made photograph which is prominently displayed, a biographical article in our monthly newsletter, and verbal commendation at periodic companywide meetings.

☐ Our supervisors are specifically trained to "serve" their employees: facilitating, not demanding; coaching, not bossing; teaching, not criticizing. We keep a very flat organizational structure with a total of four levels to encourage lateral transactions and discourage hierarchy.

☐ We try to do lots of listening—the most important aspect of communication. We regularly survey customers. Employees meet in "roundtables" with management to discuss key issues, keeping us from being content with the status quo.

Serving—a Powerful Force

Posturing the enterprise toward service takes work. Most of us would rather be served; serving others often cuts across the grain. But for those companies and individuals who make the effort, the results can be dramatic.

I saw an impressive example of this during a business meeting held at the Ritz Carlton Hotel in Palm Springs, California. Noticing the exceptional courtesy and willingness of the staff to help, I inquired of the manager: "How do you achieve this with your people?"

He pulled from his pocket the principles by which the Ritz hotels are managed and explained the extensive training that surrounds these principles. He then made a fascinating statement.

"Mr. Beckett," (he had somehow managed to learn my name!) "when we came to this valley a few years ago, there was hardly any notion of customer service. Now it seems to be everywhere, from the fast-food restaurant to the auto repair shop. People are asking what they can do to help and are following up on the quality of their service. I believe we planted some seeds that are sprouting all over. It's very gratifying."

Guess where I'd like to stay when I return to Palm Springs!

The concept of serving is a powerful force, especially when motivations are sincere and in keeping with the biblical root. The truths of Jesus' example are relevant today—in our individual lives and in the workplace. They are emulated when leadership puts on the mantle of the servant. They are nurtured by those who put others first, who—with warmth and sincerity—provide and keep providing extraordinary service.

17

Giving
Something
Back

As I WRITE, my career in business is approaching forty years. In that time, by God's grace and with enormous support from my business colleagues, family and friends, we have been able to build one of the premier mid-sized companies in America. If I compare where we are now with when I joined the company, our revenues have increased nearly 100 times (of course, a good chunk of that has been inflation). We have achieved a reputation for integrity and excellence and have been rewarded with high market share and very loyal customers. We're grateful that we've been consistently profitable and have operated with minimal debt.

This has provided us the opportunity to "give something back." In this chapter I will discuss our approach to giving, and I'll explain some of the thinking that underlies what we do. (I confess a certain reluctance to discuss our giving, in that we have chosen to keep these practices low-profile and private.)

Helping Others

Resources generated by the business have regularly been "recycled" back into the company's ongoing growth and development. We have also shared our profits with our employees on a systematic basis, through bonuses and a formal profit sharing plan. But we feel especially privileged to have been able to help others by supporting a wide array of worthy organizations that are making a real difference in people's lives, both in the U.S. and abroad. We indeed see this as an important aspect of our corporate purpose.

Locally, we've been able to help disadvantaged people get a fresh start in their work careers (Advent Industries, mentioned earlier), address systemic problems in our community in education and leadership development, and promote the preservation and beautification of natural resources in our area with both personal involvement and financial support. Overseas, we've provided funding to dig water wells in India, start micro enterprises in Africa and Central America, and address devastation from flood and famine. We see ourselves as a source of supply to those on the front line.

We also focus on activities with which we have a clear affinity—and ones we feel are able to make the greatest impact. For example, twenty-five years ago I helped found Intercessors for America, and I currently serve as its chair. This organization encourages prayer for America and its leaders in the belief that our nation must be sound spiritually if it is to prosper in other ways. IFA is regularly in touch with more than 50,000 people and 5,000 churches across the country. We now have counterparts in nearly forty nations around the world.

So as a corporation, with the full support of our board and shareholders, we've chosen to reach out to others—allocating a portion of our financial resources, but also encouraging our employees to become involved in the community. Some would call it "corporate citizenship." I can appreciate that not every business will be able to do this or will see such an approach as appropriate. Certainly it is more difficult in publicly traded companies, although many are generous in their help to others and still do very well financially. Each business must decide for itself what is the right plan.

Key Stewardship Decisions

I believe the success we've experienced and our resulting capacity to help others can be traced to some key stewardship decisions made over the years.

As you may recall from earlier in the book, I had to decide whether to stay in business or pursue activities which I thought were more directly ministry-related. I concluded I had a legitimate "calling" to business. But I felt it couldn't be just any business. It needed to reflect the highest and best of what business could be. It also became very clear to me that it wasn't really my business—it was God's. Instead of "owning" it, I was set in place as a steward, watching over it as long as God desired. Thus, as the principal shareholder, my name is on the stock certificates, but there is an "unwritten side agreement" that the business belongs to God—for indeed, it can't belong to both of us!

We've reflected our stewardship philosophy in our Corporate Roadmap as follows:

We are not an end in ourselves but a part of God's larger purposes. As such, we are called upon to work as unto Him and to be wise and able stewards of the trust He has placed with us. We realize we are dispensable at any time in God's economy, but that it is also possible to conduct ourselves in such a way as to please Him, and find His continuing favor. In other words, our work is the Lord's, and as such, *all* of our resources belong to him.

The second key stewardship decision is more personal. There was a point, fairly soon after I began to take my faith seriously, when Wendy and I decided to follow the biblical idea of tithing. Tithing is the setting aside of at least 10 percent of pre-tax income for the support of individuals and organizations doing God's work. As a family we promptly began this practice, and we were soon able to go well beyond the "tenth" in our giving. This single decision has been one of our family's greatest privileges, and at the same time the source of God's blessing on our stewardship.

But it's important to keep a clear perspective on giving and receiving. It is wrong to think we can manipulate God through our charitable giving, attempting to "twist his arm" to receive his blessings. And yet God has established a relationship between sowing and reaping. The Bible says, "As we sow, so shall we reap." I can attest that in the years following those commitments, the Lord has continued to multiply the resources he has given us to steward.

A Major Theme
The concept of stewardship is a major theme in the Scriptures,

with many applications to occupations and business. Note in these examples how much God expected of men and women.

Adam and Eve, the first man and woman, were set into a garden and given full responsibility to tend it.

Joseph was brought out of slavery and imprisonment to steward Egypt's grain supply through a devastating seven-year drought, saving countless lives throughout that vast region.

The people of Israel were given stewardship responsibility for God's revelation of himself, including his law and promises. As they were faithful in watching over this trust, they prospered. When they were not, the blessings were removed and they suffered great hardship.

Jesus taught extensively concerning stewardship, using parables set in the business context of his day. In one, recorded by Luke, a nobleman entrusted significant wealth to his servants while he went to a distant country. "Do business until I come," he said. He expected them to produce a return on the amounts they had been given. When he came back, he rewarded those who did make a profit. Those who did not lost what they had to those who were productive. They had the wrong idea of stewardship.

The New Testament word which is translated "steward" is *oikonomos,* from which we also get the word "economy." *Oikos* means "house," and *nemo* means "to arrange." It portrays the concept of administration. What we administer is not ours; it is only entrusted to us.

Finally, there is an eternal dimension to stewardship, for it is clear in various Scripture passages that we will need to give an account. In Jesus' parable about the unjust steward, the point of the lesson is the need for faithfulness: "He who is faithful in what is least is faithful also in much." Interestingly, the "least" in this case is money. There is so much more than money for which we are expected to be faithful!

What Is That in Your Hand?

Each of us has been given some measure of stewardship responsibility. Often it's so obvious we can't see it. This was so with Moses. God called him to plead with Pharaoh to let Moses' people, the Israelites, go free from their captivity in Egypt. Moses protested, so daunting was the prospect of confronting Egypt's hardened, proud ruler.

Then God asked Moses: "What is that in your hand?" In Moses' eyes, the rod he held in his hand was merely a shaft of wood, used for steadying himself during his four decades in the rocky desert of the Sinai Peninsula. In God's eyes, it was something altogether different.

"Cast it on the ground," God said.

Moses watched in utter amazement as the rod he had thrown down was transformed into a serpent. God was showing Moses that what he had in his hand was an instrument representing God's power and authority.

When it comes to seeing what we have been given to steward, we can rightfully ask, "What do I have in my hand?" To answer that question, we must see beyond money, important though that is. The resources God has given us to steward extend into many areas. For example, businesses have people. Do we maximize their potential through nurturing and challenging them? Do we help identify giftings and callings and provide opportunities for growth?

Businesses also have influence. Do we use the platforms we've been given to better our communities, to speak out on important issues and to affect public policy?

And yes, businesses have financial resources. Do we apply them wisely to add value for shareholders, employees and customers? Are some of these resources used to help those who are beyond our corporate borders—people less fortunate, those with great needs? Are we conscious of where God wants these resources to be directed to further his eternal purposes?

Larry Burkett, a widely followed financial advisor, tells the story of a first-time visitor to the U.S. He came from a less developed country where he and his friends had to trust God for provision even in the smallest things. After spending time here, he had this comment: "It is amazing to me how much can be accomplished in this nation without God!"

If this is true, we are seriously impoverished and don't know it, for it means we have ignored the foundation of all stewardship. Reality is rooted in the biblical perspective that everything we have and everything we accomplish of real value comes from God. His provision is placed with us in trust. We are his stewards.

18

The
Balancing
Act

MAINTAINING BALANCE BETWEEN work and family is one
of the most challenging tasks for a person in business.

This was driven home to me during a bittersweet discussion
among twelve leaders of major U.S. companies with whom I
recently met to forge a network for mutual strengthening and
support.

We spent time highlighting the most pressing issues we face
as Christians in business. Advertising policies, terminations,
freedom to share one's faith, and working for an unscrupulous
boss were all noted. But the most critical, by common consent,
was the challenge of raising and relating to our children.

To the credit of these busy CEO's, home-related difficulties
were set ahead of problems at work. But it was sobering to hear
story after story of serious family upheaval. These were people
who loved their children and would do anything for them. Yet

there was so much alienation, so much tension expressed, that we could only wonder what could be done—how these problems could be resolved or avoided in the first place.

We candidly acknowledged that our success in business could never compensate if our families were falling apart. But we also knew there were no easy answers.

Common Challenges

The conflicts we identified are replicated throughout corporate America, from executive suites to the plant floor and everywhere in between. The words of the prophet Malachi come to mind, the final passage in the Old Testament. He spoke of a day when the hearts of the fathers would be turned to the children and the hearts of the children to their fathers. Every father and mother reading this book yearns for that day.

As parents of six children, Wendy and I have had major challenges in childrearing. There's a long list of things we would like to do over. We can empathize with the couple who had six theories about raising children—but no children. Later they were parents with six children—and no theories!

Yet we can say that God has been very faithful to us. We've been blessed with healthy family relationships, and, as our children grow older, their friendships with each other are actually strengthening. (We honestly wondered if it would ever happen!) We are grateful they have maintained high moral standards, taken their faith seriously, and established a good sense of direction in their personal and professional lives. In fact, I felt such appreciation for them following the business leaders' meeting mentioned earlier that I wrote each a letter, telling them how much their love and exemplary character has meant to Wendy and me.

Focusing on the Family

But it's not easy to make our families a top priority. How *do* we as busy people in business achieve the balance—for ourselves and for our employees? I share a few thoughts with the sober reminder that these lessons come as much out of our failures as our successes. (Remember the six theories?)

Acknowledge the family as foundational. God sanctions three "institutions" in Scripture: family, the church and government. The church is comprised of families and will be only as sound and effective as the families within it. Governments are instituted to ensure liberty and security for both the family and the church.

Of the three, the family is primary and foundational. It was created by God, and we are set into families by God. It exists as a unit secured by love and is life's basic training ground. The promise to Abraham, the father of our faith, was that in him *all* the families of the earth would be blessed, and the results of that promise extend to us. There *is* a blessing which God wants to bestow on families!

Affirm the priority of family over work. Our priorities should be ordered like this: First, our relationship with God; then commitment to family; and only then commitment to our work and vocations. Placing our faith first will enable us to function in a godly way toward both our family and our work. But for many, this priority structure is reversed, and work takes precedence over faith and family. Most of us don't intend this to happen, but the tyranny of work overwhelms us. We neglect the home front and awaken to the grim reality that our families are adrift and rudderless in storm-tossed seas.

The choices we must make between work and family can be exceptionally difficult. The demands of work seem to be intensifying as companies "downsize" and increase expectations on those who remain. Unfettered pursuit of profits can blur other priorities. More and more, women are the family breadwinners or have to work to supplement their husbands' income and to make ends meet. If a family is under siege, achieving the time needed with spouses and children may require one or both parents to scale back hours at work or even change employment. The job that totally consumes us day in and day out can hardly be the right job.

Maximize the value of the time spent with family. Here are some specific ways we have found that our family can increase the quality of our relationships:

☐ Express love openly, and show responsible affection.

☐ Maintain a disciplined atmosphere, but balanced with good fun.

☐ Seek harmony between husband and wife—it fosters children's security.

☐ Work at communication. Be available when a family member needs to talk.

☐ Carve out regular one-on-one time with children, especially in larger families.

☐ Try to sit together at meals. Kindle wholesome mealtime conversations.

☐ Take vacations together. Center activities around the children where possible.

☐ Go easy on time-consuming personal activities during child-rearing years. (I laid aside the golf clubs for two decades—and my handicap shows it!)

☐ Attend the children's school plays and concerts; visit with their teachers. Cheer your kids on at athletic events. It's impossible to overstate the emotional effect on a child when the parents are on the sidelines at the soccer game—or are too busy to come.

☐ Limit TV. What you watch, watch together. Look for alternatives that are healthy and fun. When TV offers nothing worth watching in your family's time slot, choose a worthwhile video instead.

☐ Pray regularly—for the family and with the family.

I'm absolutely convinced the common denominator and most essential element is quality time together. As an experiment, you might ask your children what they want most. My guess is they will say time with Mom and Dad.

Family-Oriented Approaches for Business

Business leaders have the opportunity to foster and promote policies and practices that help produce healthy families. Often these are small things, not very costly, and always well received. Here are a few thoughts:

Travel policies. Limit the nights people who travel must be away. Don't insist, as some do, on travel over Saturdays to take advantage of reduced air fares.

Maternity. Make it easy for mothers to be at home with their newborn babies—the longer the better. Look for creative ways to make this possible.

Open houses and company visits. Invite children to come on a special day, and let parents show them where and with whom they work. Most young children have no idea about their parents' jobs; they simply see Mom or Dad disappearing and reappearing each day from that unpleasant thing called "work."

Company newsletters mailed to the home. Family-oriented content, including human interest stories, will build bridges between family and the workplace.

Hiring family and relatives. Yes, there are risks, but there are also rewards. Most of our experiences in hiring family have been positive. Maintain some safeguards, like not having family members report to each other.

Finding the right balance between work and family is the key, but admittedly it is not easy. Our nature is to press in one direction until we crash into a wall. Wisdom is to see the wall coming and adjust, bringing our lives into balance before it's too late.

Making the Choice

In closing this chapter on balancing family and work, let me tell you about Ed. Ed worked in maintenance for a major auto manufacturer, where he typically put in seventy hours or more each week. You can imagine his income! I met Ed at a church function, and some time later he phoned me.

"John," he said, "I need help. I'm in a job that's eating me alive. I'm making good money, but there's hardly time to enjoy it. The main problem is I simply don't have time with my wife and two sons, and I am starting to see the effects."

Generally, I'm reluctant to employ a person when it involves paying them less than they made at their previous job. In those cases, it's usually just a matter of time before they become discontented. But with Ed I was hearing a heart-cry. I saw someone who was trying to bring his priorities into line with God's. He had counted the cost.

We hired Ed, and he has been a wonderful contributor to the company as well as a close friend. He once told me that wild horses couldn't drag him back to his other job, in spite of the greater income it offered.

For the first time he felt whole. His life was in balance.

19

The
Corporate
Counselor

*T*HIS BOOK IS ABOUT THE VALUES, the principles, the habits that bring success in business. But it's not just about generic values. It centers not on a list but on a Person—one who wants more of a place in our lives. God wants a greater role not only with individuals, not just in church, but also in our families, our schools, in government, *and* in commerce and industry. He has a purpose for us and for our work and a dynamic role to play.

For God to have greater access, we must open spiritual doors—doors that invite and encourage his presence. We open those doors through personal faith and prayer.

I see indications around the globe that business people are coming to see this important truth: "When we work, we work; when we pray, God works."

My first understanding of the role of prayer for my work came early in my career at the Beckett Corporation. Dad had worn most of the hats in our small business, and after his passing I quickly realized I couldn't begin to fill all his varied roles. We had fine products, but to strengthen the company and grow, we would have to increase sales and broaden our customer base. I needed to hire a capable person, ideally someone with marketing ability.

I did what I knew to do. I sought out former college classmates and contacted people in our industry. Each was polite, but all firmly responded that they were not available. I can't blame them. We were a risky prospect.

I was only beginning to understand prayer, but the urgency of our need compelled me to reach earnestly toward God. My appeal was simple but sincere. I asked if he would please send someone to help us. The answer came remarkably soon, and in a way I didn't expect.

A Key Answer to Prayer

The Standard Oil Company of Ohio (Sohio) had recently become a customer of ours, and Bob Cook, one of their marketing execs, was asked to evaluate a company in Georgia from whom Sohio wanted to buy warm-air furnaces. He asked that I travel with him to assist in the evaluation. As we flew home following a successful visit, Bob tactfully but directly raised the subject.

"John," I recall Bob saying, "would you be open to discussing my coming to work for you? I like what I'm doing at Sohio, but I've just finished my MBA, and I believe I'm ready for a new challenge. I think I could bring some skills that would help your company move forward." I replied that I would be glad to pursue this, and over the next few weeks we worked out the details. Soon

Bob and I were working together, with Bob focusing on our marketing needs.

It didn't take me long to affirm that Bob was God's answer to prayer. In the ensuing years, his skills and personality have been an ideal complement to mine, and he has been singularly committed to our success. We have now worked in an extraordinary relationship for over three decades.

This early experience in prayer taught me an important lesson. I had exhausted my own ideas and best efforts on how to solve the problem, and only then turned to God in prayer. Even though it was clear God came to my rescue in response to that prayer, what I realized, after seeing his provision, was that I could have sought his help at the beginning.

But why pray if God already knew what our company needed? I began to see that he has designed it so that dialogue is important. And that's really what prayer is—talking with God. He wants hearts that are tender and open to his instruction—eager to know what *he* wants—not presumptuous or hard. Prayer softens the heart, attunes our hearing and affirms our dependence on God.

A Significant Factor

Prayer is not often listed in books on how to run a business. But prayer has been a significant factor in our business, not only in the crisis, but as an ongoing process. For over twenty-five years I have met every Thursday morning with a small group of men, including Bob. During these times we read Scripture, pray together and have breakfast. The prayer time often focuses on our work, including employee needs, wisdom in hiring decisions, insights into problems we are encountering, and the need for clarity on important business issues—as well as family needs and other matters that spontaneously emerge as topics for prayer.

It is especially rewarding to see answers to prayer. I recall that following the oil embargo of 1979, this group sought direction from God on what our company's response should be. Against compelling evidence that we were in for a tough time, we felt he was showing us to take one day at a time, keep our focus on him and watch for his provision. With this insight we avoided over-reacting and kept a very steady course until the storm passed. This strategy proved tremendously effective, and our company actually emerged stronger after this severe challenge.

Prayer and Work

Here are some other ways prayer and our corporate life intersect:

☐ Not infrequently, an employee makes known a personal difficulty, for example with a health or family issue. Not once have I been declined when I've asked, "Would you mind if I prayed for you and your situation?"

☐ We like to begin company events such as dinners and special gatherings with prayer. Our employees appreciate the tone this approach sets and are glad to participate.

☐ A number of years ago, we were having an unexplained rash of fires in the company. I extended an open invitation to employees to gather for prayer following work. About one-quarter of our workforce joined in petition to God for his provision and protection. Remarkably, that was the last of the fire incidents! As a friend reminded me at the time, "When we pray, coincidences happen; when we don't pray, the coincidences stop happening."

☐ On occasion a simple grace at the beginning of a business meal is appropriate. Such prayer can change the direction of the conversation, as happened with a prominent businessman who unexpectedly opened up right after a prayer of thanks for the food, revealing a family problem and his need for help.

☐ Groups of our employees gather on a completely voluntary basis to study the Bible and to pray. We make facilities available for this purpose, and occasionally we receive comments on how valuable these times of fellowship are. No pressure is ever put on folks who are not interested in participating.

I am humbled to realize there are people not associated with our company who regularly pray for us. One, an elderly man named Endel, lives in Estonia. He was imprisoned in the Soviet Gulag for ten years, but in that desperate situation he became a believer in Jesus Christ. That experience transformed his life, and ever since he arises early each morning to spend several hours in prayer. We met a few years back, and when Endel learned about our business, he told us he wanted to include us in his times of prayer. I can't help but believe this selfless commitment has contributed significantly to the blessings we see day by day.

Taking Faith Seriously

The ABC News piece featuring our company also showed the breadth of people's efforts across our nation to integrate their spiritual lives with their work. Peggy Wehmeyer and her crew visited groups of business men and women meeting in various cities for Bible study and prayer. They looked in on a group of

Jewish businessmen on Wall Street who gather weekly to read the Torah and to pray. They reported on the impact of business groups, including the Christian Business Men's Committee and the Fellowship of Companies for Christ. Thousands meet regularly in these and other organizations to explore the relationship of their faith to their work and to pray together.

I'm finding networks of senior business leaders, including heads of some of America's largest companies, who take their faith seriously. In fact, I am a member of one group which meets periodically and follows up with telephone conference calls, keeping each other in touch, praying for one another.

There is a similar emphasis internationally. The Full Gospel Business Men's Committee has chapters in every corner of the globe, and the International Christian Chamber of Commerce, based in Sweden, holds seminars and sponsors trade shows around the world for Christian business people.

As Peter Jennings said as he introduced the story on our company, there is a "growing tendency of business leaders in America to have their personal faith make an impact in their companies."

I'm convinced this trend is intimately linked with prayer, the prayer of sincere people who have a genuine desire to see business, commerce, the professions—every aspect of our work lives—come into alignment with God and his ultimate purposes.

20

Business
Direction:
Vision

*I*S THERE A SENSE of direction in your business?"

"Are certain basic values commonly held by the people with whom you work?"

"Are they effectively communicated so that there is 'buy-in' throughout the organization?"

These probing questions were posed to our senior management team a few years ago as we met with one of our company's outside board members. As we considered each, we concluded we had a challenge before us. What we had as a written vision was sketchy and cumbersome. He put us to work. We're grateful now for his prodding, but at the time it was a much larger task than we expected.

We realized through this effort that it is not enough to have vague ideas of direction in the minds of a few key executives. The company's vision and values need to be thought through, written out, then brought to life for others in the business. Vision is the focus of this chapter; values, the next.

Two Compelling Visions

Vision is the big picture, describing the destiny of an undertaking. Here are two compelling examples formulated by former heads of state.

In 1960, President John F. Kennedy delivered this memorable challenge: "I believe that this nation should commit itself to achieving the goal, before this decade is out, of landing a man on the moon and returning him safely to earth."

A computer scientist with the Apollo space program describes the impact this clear, focused and demanding goal had on his colleagues:

I have never seen a group of people work with such absolute focus and fervor as these people, who saw it as their own personal mission to send astronauts to the moon. They worked incredibly long hours, under intense pressure, and they loved it. They had something that added meaning and value to their own lives, and they gave 200 percent to make it come true. (Charles Garfield, *Peak Performers*)

President Ronald Reagan was unexcelled in our time in communicating a clearly stated vision. Standing before the long-closed Brandenburg Gate and the Berlin Wall in 1987, he declared: "This wall will fall. Beliefs become reality. You, across Europe, this wall will fall. For it cannot withstand faith; it cannot withstand truth. The wall cannot withstand freedom."

Never mind that the source of this memorable statement was

graffiti scrawled on the wall itself. President Reagan gave it life for a people yearning for change, regardless of the personal sacrifice required.

Less than two years later the wall came down. Soon after, communism's seventy-year totalitarian legacy ended (Peter Hannaford and Charles D. Hobbs, *Remembering Reagan*).

True Direction

I believe the Bible can help those of us in business to have a clear sense of direction. In fact, one way to look at the Bible is that it is entirely about vision. It is about a holy God defining reality for men and women, calling us out of our circumstances toward his destiny—or, in the words of T. S. Eliot, "the permanent things," those which are enduring, noble, full of hope.

A proverb says: "Where there is no prophetic vision the people cast off restraint [or wander aimlessly]." Does this not vividly describe the problem so many individuals and organizations— even nations—face today? It is the picture to me of a ship whose rudder is broken—adrift without a compass, caught in a pea-soup fog! But make the rudder sure, install the compass, and we find the answer to Winston Churchill's probing question: "Why is it the ship beats the waves when the waves are so many and the ship is one?" asked Churchill. "The reason is that the ship has a purpose."

Biblical Vision: A Sense of Purpose

The Bible describes many people who were impacted by God-given vision and a sense of purpose, or who suffered greatly by its lack. Our own vision can be enlarged as we glimpse at a few examples:

☐ Abraham was called and guided by God out of a prosperous city to a promised but desolate land where he would become the father of a new nation with descendants "as populous as the stars in the heavens."

☐ Nehemiah, while exiled in Persia where he was in service to the Persian king, was told that his beloved Jerusalem was lying in ruins, prompting a bold vision for the city to be rebuilt and restored. Then he became involved in implementing the vision. "Send me," he requested of the king, "that I may rebuild it."

☐ The prophet Habakkuk was given a magnificent vision that the earth would one day be filled with the glory of the Lord. In order that the vision not be lost, God emphatically impressed him to "write the vision, and make it plain . . . that he may run who reads it."

☐ And consider Jesus. While a watching world saw ultimate defeat in the shame of the cross, Jesus saw a towering victory over Satan—and beyond the cross, life in God's eternal kingdom for all who would follow him. The book of Hebrews tells us that he endured the cross "for the joy set before him"—the vision of the victory that his suffering would accomplish.

☐ At the end of this present age, the Scriptures indicate, most people will see only disjointed and random events about them. But the apostle Paul encourages us that God will be very active in a systematic summing-up process, "gathering together in one all things in Christ, both which are in heaven and which are on earth—in Him."

These few examples should remind us of the importance of vision and encourage us that the same God who has imparted vision throughout recorded history can direct us as well.

Without a Vision . . .

But sadly, there are many accounts in the Scriptures of those who were unable to lay hold of the vision given them. Three examples make the point:

☐ Esau put his appetite ahead of destiny and sold his birthright to Jacob, his younger brother, for a mere bowl of stew. Though he pleaded to have his inheritance restored, his self-serving impulsiveness brought an irreversible result. (It is essential that our success in business never be at the expense of our soul.)

☐ King Saul, Israel's first king, quickly lost vision for the nation he was leading. Driven by fear and confusion, he instead became obsessed with destroying the remarkable young man David, who was Saul's faithful admirer and the one God had appointed as his successor to the throne.

☐ Judas Iscariot, one of the twelve disciples, was unable to grasp that the person he had followed and learned from for three years was actually God's own Son. In the end, Judas betrayed Jesus, handing him over to his persecutors for a **paltry** thirty pieces of silver.

These all had a short-term, self-serving perspective, and tragically each one failed to catch a vision for God's enduring purposes.

The Application to Business

Vision that is inspired and embraced can focus and mobilize any undertaking, including our businesses.

In the process initiated by our board member, our senior management team began a process of defining our corporate direction. In due course, we developed this statement of vision:

Our Vision is to build a family of exceptional companies— each of which serves its customers in distinctive and important ways—and each of which reflects the practical application of biblical values throughout.

This theme provides continuity of culture and commonality of purpose for our more than five hundred employees in three different but related businesses. Some key words are *build, exceptional, serve, customers, biblical values*. Using these as a foundation, we are able to reinforce the major ideas and focus that will help us all move in the same direction.

Why the Bible?
Some may question our forthright reference to *biblical values*, and for many this will not be appropriate. For ourselves (and we are a privately held company), we believe this emphasis helps set the boundaries within which we want to function. As we point out in explaining our Vision to employees, every enterprise is guided by *some* point of view, some undergirding philosophy. Our management has elected to have biblical tenets and principles serve as that guide.

Employees are not obligated to agree, though virtually all see this emphasis as wholesome and positive, governing our approach toward people, finances, policies and practices. We are careful to be inclusive of any employee's faith, making sure religious beliefs have no bearing on his or her opportunity to work with or advance in our companies; rather, we seek to view all with equal appreciation and respect.

We speak of Vision and Values, but the terms are not so important. Some refer to Mission, Goals, Plans, Objectives or use other terms. What *is* important is that statements of direction be individually tailored, generated with the thoughtful involvement of leadership and broadly communicated to those who must "walk them out" in everyday life.

Here are a few guides for formulating statements of direction:

☐ They are brief.

☐ They are in writing and available.

☐ They define the sphere of activity.

☐ They are easy to understand and remember.

☐ They inspire, calling forth commitment and energy.

☐ They are subject to change, but not without careful consideration.

☐ They are consistent with, not contrary to, the principles and values in the Scriptures.

Gaining and articulating clarity of vision is the foremost responsibility of corporate leadership. From vision comes direction, helping build the values base that shapes corporate character. This values base is the focus of the next chapter.

21

Business
Direction:
Values

*B*USINESS DIRECTION is defined not only by a clear vision but by a set of core values. If well thought out and effectively communicated, such values are a powerful means of focusing the energies of an organization. They become the channel markers guiding the corporate ship toward the fulfillment of its vision.

The key question before every person in business is "Which values?" Many are searching for answers. Sensing that our culture is losing its moral and ethical bearings, wealthy individuals have been directing some of the largest grants and bequests ever given to colleges and universities to find and impart answers to that question.

Values in Academia
As an outgrowth of the ABC broadcast, I was invited to participate in a symposium on values convened by Harvard University. The

specific goal was to explore ways in which values affect private and public institutions, including government. The day-long gathering brought together some thirty people, including faculty members from Harvard's graduate schools of business, law, government and divinity, as well as leaders from business, the media and the arts.

Peter Jennings was involved, affording the two of us an opportunity to further discuss his broadcast opener, "They are using the Bible as a guide to business." He affirmed how well the news piece had been received and shared his own view that there is a hunger for spiritual content that has been largely ignored by the major media.

Our session began as we were asked to write out and prioritize the values we hold most closely. I suppose I shouldn't have been shocked, but I was. One participant, a professor in the School of Divinity, listed as her second highest priority to be a faithful spouse, raising my opinion of the values held by at least one of this elite university's staff. The euphoria was brief, however, lasting only until she boldly explained that by faithful spouse she meant she had been "married" to the same lesbian partner for eighteen years. How differently we define values! The balance of the day, while interesting, didn't move us an iota closer to identifying just what values are paramount.

A Decline in Values?

Harvard is not alone in harboring, if not encouraging, values which are a radical departure from those traditionally held in our nation. One more example. Some years ago I attended an executive management course at Stanford University. Included was a lecture on ethics given by a senior faculty member.

In good academic fashion, the floor was opened to comment after his talk. I began my question with a supposition: "Recognizing that there has been a decline in our nation's moral values . . ."

That was as far as I got before the professor interrupted: "What do you mean, a decline?"

I began citing what, to me, were clear indicators of slippage: increased crime, higher divorce rates, rampant pornography. But he cut me off again.

"Listen," he said, becoming quite agitated. "I want us to see if there is any consensus on this. How many of you disagree with this gentleman's premise that values are declining?"

Now, this was not a class of campus radicals. The 120 executives, primarily from the West Coast, ran successful medium to large businesses. I was stunned as about 80 percent of the hands in the room shot up.

"There," he proudly proclaimed. "This proves that things are not getting worse. I think people are just more open now about what's already been going on anyway."

My sole encouragement from that encounter was that some of the minority sought me out and affirmed their own observations and concerns. One, a businessman from Switzerland, said, "John, I only take issue with one thing you said. It's not just America that is in decline. It's the entire Western world."

Core Values for Business
These experiences increased my eagerness to formulate and

communicate a set of "core values" in our company. I felt these values needed to be biblically rooted if they were to have the enduring quality that would set them apart from the moral and ethical ambivalence of our current culture. At the same time, they needed to be simple, understandable and memorable—something we could build on in our education and training efforts. We have identified these three: *integrity, excellence, a profound respect for the individual.*

The third of these, profound respect, is so key that I addressed it in chapter twelve, "Infinite Worth." (I guess I wasn't sure how long you'd keep reading. . . .) The key idea is that God attributes infinite worth to the individual, and so each person deserves our profound respect. Let us now look at the first two, especially in regard to the biblical roots of these core values.

Integrity

By definition, *integrity* means adherence to a standard of values. That which is sound, whole, complete has integrity. It can be a bridge structure, a philosophy or a person. The opposite is that which is compromised, fractured, unsound. In the biblical use, the term embraces truthfulness, honesty, uprightness, blamelessness, wholeness.

Psalm 15 describes the man or woman of integrity. The dominant character qualities of such a person are listed: he or she is one who walks uprightly, who stands for righteousness, and who speaks truth inwardly—who "swears to his own hurt and does not change." I picture someone who agrees on a handshake to sell a piece of property for a certain sum. The next day another person offers more money. The person of integrity honors the prior commitment, even though backing out would bring greater profit.

From my experience, a business person's integrity is tested regularly. We encountered such a challenge early in my career with a customer in Japan. That company's buying agent asked us for a "commission" paid to him personally on sales of our products to their company. While this was clearly a bribe in our view, we learned the practice is not uncommon in Asia. We decided to be governed by our ethical standards and refused the payment of this "commission," realizing it could cost us this badly needed business. Fortunately, it didn't. The agent's response when we refused to pay was, "Fine. I just thought I'd ask!"

Imagine what a large transfusion of integrity could do to transform the badly tarnished image of modern business. The handshake might return, replacing tortuous legal contracts. There would be no news reports on business scandals and corruption like those which have recently sent prominent business leaders to prison and rocked the foundations of some of the world's largest and most prestigious companies. Time-tested absolutes would return to replace the moral relativism which has spawned so much confusion about how to think and how to act. Employees would not be caught in the dilemma of when to and when not to lie!

Excellence

Like integrity, *excellence* is a concept rooted in the Bible. (But don't tell Tom Peters—the royalties are still pouring in from his landmark study and book, *In Search of Excellence.*)

In a little seminar we had with some sixty managers in our companies, I gave them an assignment to see how excellence is evident in the opening pages of the Bible, the first chapter of Genesis. Each one in the group was able to count seven times that God considered different aspects of what he had created—and saw that it was good. In fact, on the final day God looked at everything he had made and said it was *very* good. It was excellent!

That's important: *Everything God has created is excellent!*

While Genesis provides the first look into the nature of God, the Scriptures that follow unfold a wonder and awesomeness of God beyond description. He dwells in a realm that defies our imagination—one that is totally pure, completely free from defilement and sin, perfectly ordered and intensely beautiful.

The bottom line is that this excellence, so descriptive of God's nature and the realm in which he dwells, is to be somehow integrated into the earthly time-space realm in which we live. This is exactly what Jesus meant when he taught his disciples to pray, "Thy kingdom come, Thy will be done *on earth* as it is in heaven."

Whenever something bears the mark of God's kingdom, it will be excellent. We will never fully duplicate the perfection of the heavenly realm, but by aligning ourselves with God's ambassador to earth, Jesus Christ, we can certainly emulate it. The apostle Paul expresses this idea when he says, "Whether you eat or drink, *or whatever you do, do* all to the glory of God." This is a call to excellence.

Michael J. Fox, the talented movie actor, makes an important distinction: "I am careful to not confuse excellence with perfection. Excellence I can reach for; perfection is God's business."

A way in which we have tried to encourage the concept of excellence is to seek "continuous improvement" in all we do in our company. It's the opposite concept to "If it ain't broke, don't fix it." The continuous improvement way is, "Even if it ain't broke, find a way to make it better."

Recently the team that paints our products accepted this challenge after doing things virtually the same way for years. Working with our engineers, they developed system improvements that increased productivity by over 40 percent. Now they're at it again, finding ways to improve paint quality while reducing emissions going into the atmosphere. Tomorrow we trust they'll have some additional new ideas.

Excellence. Ultimately it is defined not by a product or a process but by a person.

Jesus the Carpenter

Have you ever thought about the way Jesus began his professional career? He was a small businessman, a carpenter. Let's think of him that way for a moment, not as a religious leader. I have a large contemporary charcoal drawing of Jesus, the carpenter, over the old roll-top desk in my office. He has a simple box plane in his rugged, powerful hand, his exacting eye looking over the work he is doing. As I look at that drawing, I think about what must have been the extraordinary quality of his craftsmanship— even with the ungainly tools of that day.

I sometimes imagine him putting the finishing touches on a cabinet he has made for an elderly widow who lives down the street from his modest shop. He will deliver it to her this afternoon. She invites him in for a visit; they chat, and she is quite amazed at the breadth of his knowledge and his fine manner. This is not an ordinary carpenter, she thinks, as he goes on his way.

She walks over to the cabinet. It is very reasonably priced, she concludes, especially for such an outstanding piece. Though her eyesight is failing, she examines it closely, running her hand back and forth, up and down. It is as close to perfect as anything she has ever owned. The joints, the fit, the finish are exquisite. She can't wait to show it to her neighbors. She concludes, "The work of this carpenter, this neighbor of mine, is truly excellent."

Jesus represents excellence—his craftsmanship while here on earth merely a reflection of his enduring, impeccable character, his nature, his life and mission.

PART FOUR

The Wrap-Up

22

Loving
Monday

IN A FEW MINUTES, your plane will be touching down, taxiing to the gate, and you'll be on your way, having completed this book.

You may have wondered, *Why the title* Loving Monday?" Let me tell you the story.

As the manuscript neared completion, my editor, Dick Leggatt, and I were visiting publishers. On one trip, we had completed a busy day and were about to board a Southwest jet back to Cleveland. It was Friday afternoon, the flight completely full—mostly with weary business travelers.

"Hold on there," the flight attendant called out from inside the plane. "What are you two guys doing with your ties on? Whaddya think this is—a Delta flight?"

Dick and I grinned, gave a yank on our ties and said, "No way. We're heading home for the weekend."

Once we were shoehorned into our seats and airborne, the

Southwest attendants continued to engage the passengers in light banter. Everyone was fair game, and everyone enjoyed it. The flight crew was making their work fun—providing quality service, complying with FAA rules, but injecting some lightheartedness into the wind-up of the business week for those 120 homeward-bound business travelers.

En route, Dick and I discussed book titles. We'd already considered almost a hundred possibilities without finding just the right one. "Dick," I said, "I think this is the hardest part of this whole writing project!"

"Whoa, Bessie," bellowed the flight attendant as the plane touched down. Laughter rippled up and down the aisles.

"That flight was actually enjoyable," Dick remarked as the plane pulled up to the gate.

The next morning was Saturday. My intent was to sleep in a bit, but I couldn't. My mind turned again to the bewildering task of finding a title. One idea, then another, then another. Then it hit. *Loving Monday,* I thought. *That's it! The attendants on that flight made their work fun. If they were living for Friday, they sure didn't show it. I'll bet they love Mondays as much as I do!*

Thus the title was born. As I tried it out on others, the response was enthusiastic. But more than liking a title, they liked the idea. "I hear too many people grumble about Mondays," was a typical comment. Then they would add, "But I don't see it that way. I love Mondays. Always have."

Actually, the whole idea of work has gotten a bum rap in our Western culture. As with so many distortions from the biblical norm, we've come to associate work with drudgery and futility, not dignity and fulfillment. But an esteemed place for work was actually initiated by God himself, the one who right from the first verse of the Bible was committed to work—creating the heavens and the earth, then sustaining everything he created. But God also knew how to rest. "And on the seventh day God ended His work which He had done, and He rested," says the Genesis account. Created as we are in the image of God, it's almost as though men and women were made to work, then judiciously to rest. It's like a rhythm, built into the human cycle of life. Both are important, even essential.

I think of this intended cycle as I remember George, a hard-working employee who started with our company just after World War II. He had seen the worst of the war in the Pacific as a seaman in the U.S. Navy. Somehow the disciplines he'd learned carried over to his job as an assembler of oil burners. Remarkably, when he retired after nearly thirty years, George had not missed a single day of work. Sure, he'd had some minor illnesses and occasionally had to fight bad weather to get to work. But he was there. George was always there, *almost* always healthy.

But then, with his retirement, he stopped working. At first he would still get up at five, just the way he used to. But before long he began sleeping in. George became bored with his life. Within months, illnesses cropped up and left him debilitated. Then discouragement hit. He'd lost his sense of purpose. A key aspect of his life was gone. Sadly, within a few years George died, missing most of the retirement he had anticipated for so many years. His work had become a more vital part of his life than he or anyone else realized.

Key Concepts

One of the purposes of this book is to give you a fresh zeal for your work—both now and in future years. In summary, here are some of the key concepts which undergird truly rewarding work and vocation.

Work is a high calling, not secondary in value. We should endeavor to stay within our areas of gifting, in the spheres we've been allotted. Work takes on added dignity as we regard each person we contact in business with great respect, and as we function in a framework of excellence and integrity. It is essential that our success never be at the expense of our soul—there *is* more to consider than the bottom line. The norms and values rooted in the Bible can serve as a compass in this regard, on seas that can be turbulent and treacherous.

A sense of purpose emerges as we look for opportunities to serve one another in our work, and as we strive to be responsible stewards of resources committed to our care. Our vocations are much more apt to be a delight when our priorities are right, with proper place given to our relationship with God and with our families. We will find that we can have peace in the most incredibly difficult work situations when we commit our ways to the Lord and give time to prayer. And, perhaps most of all, we can be energized by a bold and lively vision for what we're doing—a vision that provides direction and draws us up into that which is noble and worthy.

And yet there is a dimension that goes beyond the most carefully crafted guidelines to business success. It is to this dimension that we now turn.

23

The
Ultimate
Goal

VISION . . . MISSION . . . PURPOSE . . . principles . . . values . . . goals . . . strategies . . . objectives . . .

It can all be rather overwhelming.

A major purpose of this book is to present the relevance of a biblical approach to business. It is to affirm that we can find practical insights, answers and direction through knowing and applying the inexhaustible treasures found in the Bible—that timeless book that graces the bookshelf in your home.

But even the clearest exposition of biblical truth and the most zealous efforts to integrate this truth into our work will leave us short of the ultimate goal. *The ultimate goal is a relationship.*

Sometimes the common things that happen during the day help me to understand important truths.

I like to run—or should I say jog—but not as much as Chamois, our golden retriever. When he sees my running shoes go on in the morning, he goes ballistic. He's well trained and runs without a leash. He likes to get out ahead twenty or thirty yards and take small detours to sniff this or that.

What I've noticed is the way he frequently glances back toward his master. It's just a quick turn of the head, but it's enough to recalibrate, to alter the pace or the direction.

One day it occurred to me that the Lord was using this simple example to nudge me toward such a relationship with him, one where I would stay close, frequently check in and be careful not to stray off.

Staying in Touch

The message of the gospel is that we are invited into a real, vital and personal relationship with God. Jesus refers to it as *abiding*, in the sense of dwelling together over a long period of time. He amplifies, using the analogy of how branches are intimately linked to and grow out of a vine: "I am the vine, you are the branches."

This relationship is essential to all of life, including our capacity to extend biblical truth into the workplace. It transcends principles, as lofty as those principles may be. I emphasize this because principle-based literature often stops short of the fundamental importance of relationships.

Let me use an analogy.

I have a wonderful relationship with my wife, Wendy. We've known each other for more than forty years. It is uncanny how much we understand each other, how we know what the other is thinking without a word being spoken. Our love relationship has carried us through the challenge of raising six children, working through the deaths of loved ones, facing serious illnesses and accidents, standing together as our business was built, overcoming the strains, temptations, misunderstandings and adversity every married couple encounters.

But did we do it by following carefully scripted principles? Of course not.

A relationship is fluid—it goes beyond adherence to principles. It prospers when there is time taken together, when there is intimate conversation, when joys and sorrows are shared, when difficulties are worked through. If carefully tended, it grows and becomes the dearest thing in life.

A Unique Closeness

What applies in close relationships with loved ones is even more essential in our relationship with God.

The ultimate goal (and privilege) in life is to know God intimately—and this happens as we establish and maintain a personal relationship with Jesus Christ.

Out of that relationship flows not only the truth but also the means to properly handle that truth. Out of knowing God comes the capacity to sit in God's presence—in his private office—every day, to gain his perspective and learn his ways. Knowing God means our life becomes filled with his life.

In his book *Experiencing God,* Henry Blackaby has helped me understand the unique relationship that each of us can have with God the Father through Jesus Christ. Blackaby says we experience God when we follow the pattern modeled by Jesus.

Jesus said, "My Father has been working until now, and I have been working." Blackaby draws a remarkable insight from this verse: "God is presently at work all around us—in situations, in circumstances, in difficulties. He is continually active, always with His ultimate purposes in mind."

Jesus saw it as his responsibility to watch what his Father was doing and to join in. He said, "The Son can do nothing of Himself, but what He sees the Father do; for whatever He does, the Son also does in like manner. For the Father loves the Son, and shows Him all things that He Himself does."

Here is the pattern for us—to understand that God is at work all around us and in our lives, and to *join with him in what he is doing!*

The key is a close, ongoing relationship. It is more than attending a church service and then going off to do our thing during the week. It is different from waking in the morning, having a time of Bible reading and prayer and then plunging into the day in our own strength. It is keeping our eyes on the Master, watching closely, discerning where and how he is active and then following him.

Our ultimate goal goes beyond knowing *about* God and his principles. Our ultimate goal is to come to know him as our Maker, Redeemer and Friend. Amazingly, God wants that kind of intimate relationship with us! It is the most precious of all possible gifts.

Bud
One day Bud came to grips with his need for a more intimate relationship with the Lord.

Bud joined our company in the late sixties as a department

supervisor, and after several years he progressed to plant super-intendent, serving as a member of our senior management team. He held that position until his retirement, nearly twenty years after he began working with us.

An ex-Marine and a veteran of World War II with extensive combat duty in the Pacific, Bud was a no-nonsense boss whose tough exterior masked a tender heart. Nonetheless, his iron-grip handshakes let others know who was in charge.

Shortly before retirement, Bud was hospitalized with a bron-chial infection. As I entered his hospital room for a visit, I sensed an anxiety in Bud that was uncharacteristic. Gone was the confident "I'm-still-in-charge" demeanor.

I had hardly said hello when Bud grimaced, revealing his pain, then blurted out, "John, I'm worried."

"Look," I said, "they'll get on top of this infection in no time. With the new antibiotics . . ."

But he cut me off. "No," he said, "that's not my concern. I've been doing some thinking since I got in here, and I'm not sure things are right between God and me."

"Bud," I said, adjusting to his unexpected comment, "you and I have worked together a long time. You've seen my struggles over the years. But you've also heard me say my faith has helped me through those struggles."

"Yeah, I've been watching," Bud injected, squeezing out a wry smile. "I hate to admit it, but I've poked fun at your faith from time to time. For myself, I've never said much about what I believe. It's always been more of a private matter."

"Okay," I said. "Let me ask you a direct question. If you could, would you like to be more certain of your relationship with the Lord?"

Never one to mince words, Bud was equally direct in his response. "I would," he said, "I really would."

So we talked about the basics of the Christian faith—how sin has separated us from God, and how Jesus died for us on the cross, providing a way for our relationship with God to be restored—if we are willing.

I could understand his reserve. It hadn't been that many years since I was working through the same issues. And now it was Bud pressing further. "So what do I do?" he asked.

"The key is for you to put out the welcome mat. The Lord is gracious, and he isn't going to force you to do anything. But if you ask him, he is more than willing to come to you. Believe me, he will become the closest friend you've ever had."

The Lord became Bud's friend that day. His prayer of acceptance was simple, but it came from his heart. "John," he said, his eyes now misty, "I turn sixty-four next month, and this is probably the most important thing I've ever done."

That day, Bud anchored his faith in a way he never had before. His decision became the basis for his ongoing personal relationship with the Lord. It is especially poignant to recall that special time together, for as I was doing the final editing of this book, Bud died. Attending the funeral service, I was wonderfully reassured to know that because of the commitment he made that day in the hospital, Bud is eternally in the presence of the Lord.

24

Business Ambassadors

OUR LIVES AND WHAT WE DO with them are important to God. A close relationship with the Lord will bring about a compelling and necessary result. We will find it possible to bring every aspect of our lives, including our work, into alignment with God's truth and design. This in turn will transform us into people who are not only more effective as human beings and as workers but more pleasing to God.

God himself, through his Word and his Spirit, provides the context within which we must operate. When we are bounded by the guidelines he establishes and the wisdom he imparts, our work will delight him and further his kingdom here on earth.

Let's peer into the future and look at God's larger agenda for a moment. Earlier I noted a vision given to the Old Testament prophet Habakkuk. In that vision he foresaw a coming day when the glory of the Lord would fill the entire earth.

"Earth," as the prophet used this word, was intended to include everyone and everything on the planet. "Glory" signifies honor, substance, renown and visible splendor—the opposite of instability, temporariness and emptiness—and actually signifies the very presence of God himself. Imagine. That kind of glory filling the entire earth. What a vision!

Right Here—Right Now

Now here is the key question. Does it not seem likely that God intends our work and occupations to be included as he immerses everything in his glory? Is this an aspect of the compelling vision the prophet saw? If this is indeed God's direction, what are the implications for us day to day? If so, is it not consistent that we would be engaging that process here and now—not waiting for the "sweet by-and-by," but doing all we can currently to align our work with God's glory?

For myself, I cannot but answer in the affirmative. From this perspective, I find each day is important and filled with opportunity. Not just to "survive the rat race," but to actually have a part, however small, in consciously knitting what I do into God's larger purposes.

In America, we are very privileged to have the freedom to integrate our faith and our work. This isn't so everywhere across the earth, and, really, we must not take it for granted in our own nation. This lesson was driven home to me a few years ago.

Contending with the EEOC

You may recall from earlier comments that a while back I found myself in the midst of a battle with the Equal Employment Opportunities Commission. It was this involvement that eventually resulted in the news piece with ABC.

The EEOC had issued some ill-conceived guidelines that would likely have imposed severe restrictions on the exercise of religious liberty in the U.S. workplace. I tell the story because the commission's approach would have directly impeded the process of aligning our work with God's design.

Dudley Rochelle, an attorney in Atlanta, was perusing a recently published *Federal Register* and saw the proposed guidelines amending the Civil Rights Act of 1964. As she read them in detail she saw some ominous implications. She quickly wrote a brief, which I received just days before the end of November 1993, the close of the sixty-day period for public comment. I wrote to the EEOC with my concerns and encouraged several of my friends in business to do the same.

But it became clear that this proposal would sail through Congress to become law, and that the letters of objection, less than ten, would have no effect. I found I was being stirred by a righteous anger that a handful of bureaucrats could possibly shut down workplace Bible studies, prayer before business meetings, the singing of carols at a Christmas dinner, the display of a poster for a church-related event, or even the wearing of jewelry with a religious symbol. Other attorneys with whom I spoke confirmed this possibility.

Preventive Measures
I was further encouraged to get involved as I read in Isaiah 28

that the Lord would give strength to "those who hold back the battle at the gate." This spoke to me of taking preventive measures now, before it was too late. I concluded that if these guidelines became law, it could take a decade to restore workplace religious liberty. By then, the damage would have been done. We learned, in fact, that a major airline had already issued instructions restricting bulletin board notices in their operations centers: any reference to religious content was forbidden.

Humanly speaking, there seemed to be no way to prevent the EEOC guidelines from becoming law. But God provided a way.

I learned that while the public could no longer comment, members of Congress could. I met with Mark Siljander, a former member of the U.S. House of Representatives, who immediately saw the dangers and jumped into the fray. He was inspired! Within weeks, and with the help of the January 1994 snowstorm that paralyzed Washington and slowed the reconvening of Congress, we were able to mount an effort to get this issue on the radar screen of several supportive members of the House and Senate.

Various prayer ministries became involved, encouraging their members to mount a nationwide crescendo of prayer that the proposed guidelines would not go through. Then Christian Broadcasting Network News got involved. Pat Robertson, never one to duck something threatening religious liberty, sent a camera crew to our company. I was interviewed for a TV story which showed activities that might have to be abandoned, including a group of our employees who had gathered for a voluntary Bible study.

The message was clear: "Such activities as these may not be

possible in the future!" This hit the national airwaves in repeated showings. Interviews on radio talk shows ensued, then special coverage by Dr. James Dobson on his "Focus on the Family" broadcast. Now the ball was really rolling.

An Outpouring of Support

Major network TV news programs picked it up, and the *Wall Street Journal* wrote a hard-hitting article for which I was interviewed. Congressional offices were besieged with mail and phone calls. People wrote over 100,000 letters of protest to the EEOC, more than ten times the number they had received on any previous issue. Practically no one wrote in support!

An amusing incident occurred during this process, reminding me of the Lord's sense of humor. A coalition was invited to meet with EEOC attorneys to discuss the guidelines. We were strange bedfellows, with representatives ranging from the conservative National Association of Evangelicals to the liberal American Civil Liberties Union. The meeting was cordial but combative. As I was leaving the EEOC headquarters in Washington, I noticed a beautiful poster in an office cubicle with a verse from the Bible on it. I couldn't resist drawing one of the EEOC attorneys aside to point out to her that under their proposal it might have to be taken down. Her knowing nod confirmed that the point had been made.

Freedom Preserved

A resolution was introduced into the U.S. Senate to cut off funding to the EEOC for the promulgation of their guidelines, and in a rare display of unity, the Senate voted 100 to 0 for passage! Soon after, the House of Representatives followed with an overwhelming, though not unanimous, vote. Faced with this wall of resistance, in the fall of 1994 the EEOC withdrew the guidelines.

It was a tremendous victory—an affirmation to me that the same God who created the far-flung heavens also cares about our having the uncontested freedom to voice matters of faith in the workplace.

It was also a wake-up call to us in business that our liberties must not be assumed. The EEOC challenge brought us within a razor's edge of a government mandate that could have cost us these liberties forever. This battle confirmed to me that we in business need to be bold in the exercise of the freedoms we have, to declare and act on our beliefs.

It is an aspect of the commission Jesus gave his followers to be "salt" and "light."

Salt and Light

On one of my visits to Israel, I was able to stand where it is believed Jesus stood when he spoke about salt and light in the Sermon on the Mount—overlooking the beautiful hills surrounding the azure waters of the Sea of Galilee. It is a breathtaking setting. As he addressed the crowd, Jesus was no doubt mindful that in those hills beyond the sea were tens of thousands of people, tucked away in small villages, who also needed to hear his message. He implored those who were listening to take the message out to the world around them.

"You are the salt of the earth," Jesus said. "Salt" to them conveyed the idea of both a preservative and an agent to create thirst. They also realized that in the process of doing its job, salt could be an irritant. "Be salty," Jesus nonetheless admonished.

He went on: "You are the light of the world. A city set on a hill cannot be hidden. Nor do they light a lamp and put it under a basket, but on a lampstand, and it gives light to all who are in the house. Let your light so shine before men, that they may see your good works and glorify your Father in heaven."

In effect, Jesus was saying it is not enough to have a "private faith." If it is real, it needs to shine forth, challenging the darkness.

Ambassadors

The apostle Paul used a different metaphor, but one which conveyed a similar purpose, as he addressed the church in Corinth, encouraging them to reach out and make an impact upon the society around them. Corinth was a seaport, strategically located as a hub of commerce and trade for the Roman Empire, a city bustling with activity—with merchants and managers, ships' crews and captains, dockworkers and traders, soldiers and noblemen— and, on occasion, even emperors and kings.

Let me paraphrase what Paul said to his followers: "Be Christ's ambassadors to these people. He wants to reconcile every aspect of the world to himself, including these who are busily engaged in their trades, their responsibilities in business and in govern-ance. He wants to bring them and their work into alignment with his ultimate purposes. He wants to reveal to them his love, his compassion, his care. He has a destiny for them beyond what they can see. This is reality; the rest is illusory. And he wants your help! Be ambassadors!"

Loving Monday

This call extends to each of us who has decided to embrace the message of the gospel. We are salt. We are light. We are his ambassadors. In business. Where we are. To everyone with whom he brings us in contact. In the work, the vocation, to which he has called us. Using whatever platforms he provides.

For indeed, there is that day coming—a day when God's glory will envelop every atom, every plant and human cell, every family and home—and, yes, every place of work.

Let us hold this vision before us, and do all we can to hasten its fulfillment.

There is wonderful hope beyond the weekend. It involves that very special assignment to which God has called us: our work. And it begins next Monday.

Discussion
Questions

Questions for each chapter have been included in this new paperback version of *Loving Monday*. While these questions can be used for individual study and reflection, the greatest value comes from the rich give-and-take discussion that can happen in a small study group. You might think about forming such a group where you work and studying a chapter each time you get together.

I am indebted that a Colorado businessman, Rich Case, took the initiative to propose and develop these discussion questions. May they enrich your work experience and help you "love Mondays" to the fullest.

Chapter 1: Peter Jennings's Magnifying Glass

1. List a few specific ways your basic beliefs have a bearing on the way you go about your work.

2. Would you be excited or troubled if a national TV network wanted to do a story on how your faith relates to the way you do business? Why? If they could speak without restriction to anyone in your company, would they likely find

☐ an exciting story of values and faith?

☐ a troublesome story of a discrepancy between stated values and management behavior?

☐ not much of anything?

Describe the likely scenario.

3. Think about some conflicts you routinely face between walking in faith and the practical world of business. Describe one.

4. In what areas of business do you operate as if faith and work were mutually exclusive?

5. Review Nehemiah 2:17-20. Nehemiah was given the task of returning to Jerusalem after the Babylonian captivity and rebuilding the wall—certainly an ambitious business enterprise.

☐ How did he view God's role in this endeavor?

☐ To whom did his team look to for their success in completing the wall? Why?

☐ How do you think Nehemiah viewed the overlap between his deeply held beliefs and his "business assignment"?

Chapter 2: Companions for Life

1. Think about your personal history. List a few pivotal points in your life (forks in the road, key decisions, times of difficulty). How have they impacted your life and led you down certain paths to where you are today? Highlight when you came to know Christ as your Lord and Savior. (If you have not made this sure step of faith, please refer to point 4 on page 190 or pick up Lee Strobel's book *The Case for Christ* for help along your spiritual journey.)

2. Describe your pattern (your regular discipline) of Bible reading and study. Do you consider it a delight, a burden, or is it basically nonexistent? Why?

3. Review 2 Timothy 3:16.

☐ How does Paul, the author, describe Scripture?

☐ What does this expression "inspired by God" mean to you?

☐ Paul outlines why Scripture is useful. State practical examples of what each term means practically to you:

teaching

rebuking

correcting

training in righteousness

☐ What do you think is the primary purpose of studying and understanding Scripture?

☐ What does it mean that the Bible "thoroughly equip[s] us for every good work"?

☐ What is our good work as it relates to business? Think of an example.

☐ In what practical ways can we integrate faith into our daily business practices?

☐ Why is daily study of the Scriptures so important to this process?

Chapter 3: Trouble in Camelot

1. Describe a particular time of crisis or trouble that you have experienced along your life's path, especially in your work.

☐ How have you responded to such times? Why?

☐ What have you learned from crisis or trouble that can help you in the future?

2. Review Psalm 107.

☐ Of what kind of troubles does the psalmist speak?

☐ In each instance, how did the people get through their trouble?

☐ In each instance, what was God's response to their cry for help?

3. Based on these truths, list some specific ways God might want you to respond when you face trouble and stress in your work.

Chapter 4: Trial by Fire

1. Can you recall specific times when trials and difficulties either helped you to develop a dependence on God or caused you to fall into doubt and frustration? Describe one.

2. How would you define *sovereignty*? List a few things you believe about God's sovereignty.

3. Review Romans 8:28.

☐ What assurance do we have regarding God's sovereignty?

☐ What does this mean about the future of your business?

4. Review James 1:2-8.

☐ What should be our attitude toward trials?

☐ What are the purposes of trials in our life?

☐ How would you describe perseverance? Why is perseverance so important to the development of character?

☐ As we are going through trials, in what way does God want us to approach him?

Chapter 5: The Invisible Hand

1. Looking back over your life (refer to your notes from chapter two), describe a few experiences that revealed God's invisible hand at work. Were you able to recognize his activity at the time?

2. What is something you think God is nudging, prodding or encouraging you to do right now? What are your struggles and feelings about this?

3. Review Proverbs 3:5-8.

☐ What is the key to understanding God's pathway for your work, career or business?

☐ If we are willing to "not be wise in our own eyes" (not assume we know what is best), what are God's promises to us?

4. Are you willing to "let go" and trust your work or your business to God? What is necessary to push through this struggle? Name one area you will "let go of" and entrust to God this week.

Chapter 6: Strangely Warmed

1. As God is calling you into a fuller relationship with himself, what types of "death" have you personally encountered? (What specific areas, struggles or character issues have a hold on you and keep you

from moving on to freedom in the new life God offers?)

2. Review Colossians 3:1-17.

☐ On what should our minds be focused? Why?

☐ List some of the specific steps these verses tell us to take in order to put to death the parts of our character still belonging to the "earthly nature."

3. In one sentence describe your general perspective on your vocation.

4. List any struggles you may be experiencing between (1) the desire to be serving God in "ministry" activities and (2) understanding the ministry nature of your calling in your work.

5. Would you like to strengthen your commitment to your calling? Perhaps you have doubts about God's purpose for your life in business. If so, you can name those doubts and commit them to God this week.

Chapter 7: Two Worlds, or One?

1. Name one area where you tend to live in two separate worlds—the spiritual and the secular.

2. Identify the main struggle you face in trying to integrate the two.

3. Review 1 Thessalonians 4:1-12.

☐ To what does God call us?

☐ Why does he call us to this?

4. How do these verses apply to God's view of the "spiritual" and the "secular"? In what way are his purposes fulfilled by your leading an integrated life of faith at work versus living in two separate worlds?

Chapter 8: Culture Wars

1. Name a few situations where you see the workplace driven by situational ethics and expediency as opposed to absolute values and moral law.

2. In what ways have ethical dilemmas impacted your own business environment?

3. Review Psalm 19:7-14.

☐ How does the psalmist view God's law and absolute values?

☐ How does this benefit us?

☐ How do we allow "presumptuous sins" (v. 13) to creep into our daily life?

4. Is the ability to stand up for absolute truths in your business difficult for you? Why or why not?

5. What further steps do you need to take to rethink your perspective on absolute truth and its importance for integration?

Chapter 9: A Greek Legacy

1. Have you been affected by the dualistic worldview of life and business (promulgated by Greek philosophers such as Plato and Aristotle, and even by Christian theologians such as Augustine and Aquinas), which suggests that it is impossible to serve God by being in business? If so, name one or two specific examples.

2. Describe in one sentence your attitude about being a person called to business.

3. Name two areas (particularly at work) in which you tend to have the worldview of dividing life into two areas—the sacred and the secular.

4. Identify some of the sources for this thinking in your own life.

5. Review John 10:7-10.

☐ What happens when we enter through the gate (Christ) into his kingdom?

☐ What does this mean to you?

☐ When the passage says Jesus has come that you might have life and have it abundantly, what does this mean to you?

☐ Do you believe Christ wants us to view our abundant life as an integrated whole and not compartmentalized? Why or why not?

☐ Do you want to take that step of commitment? If so, list one area you will commit to change this week.

Chapter 10: A Different Window

1. In what way is dualism a hindrance to our internal peace and our effectiveness in life?

2. Review 1 Timothy 4:4-5.

☐ What has God created?

☐ What does he call them?

3. Review Genesis 1:10, 12, 18, 21, 31.

☐ What is our response to this view of the world?

4. Review 1 Thessalonians 5:16-22.

☐ Reflect on how God wishes us to see and to develop our life as an integrated whole.

5. Review 1 Thessalonians 5:23-24.

☐ What is the result of our developing our life in this way?

☐ What does all this say about God's worldview for us?

☐ What are the implications of these verses regarding how we look at life, particularly our work?

6. How may this worldview change what we think and do at work?

7. Name two benefits you expect from this change.

Chapter 11: Enduring Truth

1. Name three enduring qualities that are important to you.

2. In what ways are these qualities challenged by what you encounter in your occupation?

3. Review Daniel 6:1-28.

☐ How would you describe Daniel's vocation?

☐ Why was he promoted?

☐ What were his outstanding qualities?

☐ What happened to the "world system" around him?

☐ How did Daniel respond?

☐ What was the immediate consequence of his taking a stand on principles?

☐ What was the long-term result?

☐ If Daniel had not been rescued, would the key point of the story change? Why or why not?

4. Name one of Daniel's qualities that is missing in your life. What specific step do you feel you ought to take to build that quality? Commit to taking that step this week.

Chapter 12: Infinite Worth

1. Describe in a sentence how you tend to regard your employees or coworkers.

2. How would the people in your company describe how they are viewed by the company?

3. Is there a difference between these two perspectives? Why?

4. Review 1 Peter 2:13-17.

☐ What do you think is God's will for you?

☐ What steps have you taken in the past that have been successful in creating goodwill and showing proper respect to employees in your business? List three creative steps you could take for doing more in this area (specific policies and programs that might better encourage individuals' value and worth).

Chapter 13: Blueprints

1. Identify (in one sentence each) what you believe to be your main calling, gifting and sphere.

2. What steps are you now taking to encourage employees you work with to understand their unique destiny in God? What steps do you see as needed?

3. Name two or three benefits of providing a context for growth and

enabling employees to find and fit in with God's design for their lives.

4. Review 1 Corinthians 12:27-31 and Ephesians 4:11-12.

☐ How should we view how God has appointed each person?

☐ What is your conclusion on the basis of this passage?

☐ How does the good of the business benefit from our willingness to see people as uniquely gifted?

5. Name a way you might better promote the process of (1) identifying individuals' abilities and gifts and (2) positioning people accordingly.

Chapter 14: Trouble, Trouble, Toil & Trouble

1. Think of a time when you let anger or pride separate you from a coworker, supervisor, subordinate or someone else in your business—maybe a supplier or customer. What were the causes and how was it resolved? If unresolved, why?

2. What external circumstances threaten your business right now? How are you reacting? What is at the root of your reaction?

3. How might you develop a positive, aggressive response versus a negative, defensive one?

4. Review 1 Samuel 17:1-54.

☐ What were the circumstances threatening Israel?

☐ What was David's response to these circumstances (vv. 26, 29, 32)?

☐ What did David reject as the weapons to use in the battle, and with what "core competencies" did David defeat Goliath?

☐ What understanding of truth was at the core of David's faith (v. 47)?

☐ Give an example of how you might apply this understanding to your circumstances.

5. For further encouragement and discussion, read and meditate on Psalm 112 and 2 Chronicles 20:1-12.

Chapter 15: The Compassionate Enterprise

1. Name a situation where you had to balance biblical principles of

compassion and accountability in your business.

2. Identify two areas where you need to better balance these principles in your work environment. What steps can you take during this week to implement improvement?

3. Review Luke 10:25-37.

☐ Why were the priest and the Levite unwilling to help the man in trouble?

☐ What was the key difference in the Samaritan?

☐ How did the Samaritan respond to what he saw and felt?

4. Name a situation you are facing right now that calls for compassion.

5. How do you currently handle terminations? How might you better use compassion in this process?

6. In what areas might your company extend a compassionate hand to your community? How would your coworkers react to such an initiative?

Chapter 16: Extraordinary Service

1. Think of one possible action you could take in your position that would fall into the category of extraordinary service.

2. Does your organization have a core competency that reflects the biblical mandate of providing extraordinary service? Why or why not?

3. What are some examples? How have they benefited the business?

4. Review Mark 10:35-45.

☐ What were the disciples' personal desires?

☐ When Jesus called them together for this "group teaching moment," what did he say in regard to their desires?

☐ How would you translate this into a principle of developing extraordinary service for your company?

5. What programs do you have in place (or need to put in place) to

train your people in extraordinary service? If some training is already in place, what results are you seeing?

Chapter 17: Giving Something Back
1. In one sentence express what you believe about your company "giving something back."
2. In one sentence express your definition of, and perspective on, stewardship.
3. Review Deuteronomy 15:7-10, Proverbs 3:9-10 and Malachi 3:10.
☐ What attitude does God wish us to guard against?
☐ What attitude does he wish us to learn to enjoy?
☐ What does God promise as a result of this attitude?
☐ What challenge does God offer to us, and what does he promise if we follow through?
4. Name two or three ways you exercise the principle of generosity and maximize the potential of the resources God has entrusted to you.
5. Name one creative way you might utilize your platform in business to influence the business community for the kingdom of God. What step can you take now toward this goal?

Chapter 18: The Balancing Act
1. In what ways does your business encourage or discourage the balancing of work and family in the following areas?
☐ Acclaiming family as a foundational value
☐ Affirming priority of family over work
☐ Maximizing time spent with family
2. Review Deuteronomy 6:1-9.
☐ To what does this passage call us to be obedient?
☐ What does this mean?
☐ What steps does God expect us to take regarding our obligation to ingrain his principles in our family?

☐ What does this mean regarding balancing of work and family?

3. Think about a family-oriented approach you could introduce in your company to promote this value of balance. What would it be?

Chapter 19: The Corporate Counselor

1. What role does prayer play in your vocation? in the operation of your business? Are there regular opportunities in your company when corporate prayer might be appropriate for your employees and coworkers? Describe.

2. Do you find it a natural response to go to prayer about your daily business situations, or is it a struggle for you? If a struggle, what steps can you suggest for overcoming it?

3. Name two specific answers to prayer that you have experienced in your business.

4. Review 2 Chronicles 1:7-12 and James 1:5.

☐ When Solomon was given the opportunity to ask for anything he wanted, what did he ask for?

☐ How did God respond? Why?

☐ What should be our continual prayer for our businesses?

☐ What should you expect?

5. How might you develop opportunities to pray with others in your company about your business? What is the next step toward achieving this goal?

Chapter 20: Business Direction: Vision

1. In one sentence define your personal "compelling vision."

2. In one sentence define your company's "compelling vision."

3. In what ways do these two statements guide your business?

4. Review Nehemiah 1:1-11; 2:17-18.

☐ What was Nehemiah's compelling vision? Why was it important?

☐ How did he go about developing it?

☐ How did he communicate it?

☐ How did the people respond?

5. If you do not fully understand your company's compelling vision, how might you develop clarity?

6. Once it is clear to you (or if it is already clear), how might you promote and instill the company's vision throughout the organization? Why is this so important?

Chapter 21: Business Direction: Values

1. List two or three of your company's core values.

2. In what ways do you presently stimulate your employees to adopt and follow these values? Are further steps needed to do this better? If so, name a couple of steps that would begin the process.

3. How do you receive feedback regarding how well your executives and employees adhere to these values?

4. Review Matthew 7:24-27.

☐ What happens to something that is built on shifting, loose material versus something that is built on a solid foundation?

☐ What is the reason the strong foundation promotes survival and stability?

☐ How is building your business on core values like building on solid rock?

5. Think of a situation that challenged you to maintain your values instead of caving in to expediency. Describe.

6. At this time what is the more pressing need: for you to reestablish your core values or better promote them? Why?

Chapter 22: Loving Monday

1. List the key concepts involved in "loving Monday"—having a fresh zeal for your work. Refer to page 162.

2. Review Deuteronomy 26:16-19 and Joshua 11:15.

☐ What did God tell Moses and then Joshua to do?
☐ What was God's promise if they followed through on this?
☐ What did they do?
3. Of the concepts listed in question 1, identify one that is presently working well in your life (a success) and one that you are struggling to institute in your life and work.
☐ What steps would help you overcome the struggle? Name two.
☐ Which step will you take this week?

Chapter 23: The Ultimate Goal
1. In one sentence express God's ultimate purpose for his people.
2. Review Matthew 6:33-34.
☐ What does God wish us to have as our first priority?
☐ What does the term *kingdom* mean?
☐ How does seeking first the kingdom of God fulfill God's ultimate purpose?
☐ In what practical ways can we seek first the kingdom of God?
☐ What is the outcome of seeking God first in all we do?
☐ What types of things in our businesses can we count on God taking care of for us?
3. What specific changes in attitude or priorities do you think God is asking you to make for his ultimate purpose? Name one or two, and commit to following through on them.
4. Read over the story of Bud, beginning on page 166. Can you say with confidence that you have entered into a personal relationship with the Lord? If you cannot, you can do that now. With your heart open to receiving God's salvation, pray this prayer:

I ask forgiveness, Lord Jesus, for being separated from you, and I ask that you help me turn from my old life and come back to you.

I receive you as God's Son, the One who through your death and resurrection gives me new life. Please restore the relationship you have desired for me all along. Be my Lord.

And now, I thank you. Thank you that you hear when I call out to you; that you receive me just as I am. Thank you for allowing me to become your follower and a member of your family. Please give me strength to walk with you each day, and lead my life in ways that are pleasing to you. Amen.

Chapter 24: Business Ambassadors

1. Write your definition of the term *ambassador.*

2. Describe being an ambassador for Christ in the larger context of the business world.

3. Review 2 Corinthians 5:14-21.

☐ What should be the main motivating factor for everything we do (v. 14)?

☐ How are we to view the people around us?

☐ What is the purpose of our ministry as ambassadors?

☐ As a result of our participation in this process, what will happen to us?

4. In what specific ways do you believe God is calling you to be his ambassador in the job in which he has placed you?

5. What steps might you take to move in this direction?

Further Reading

Blackaby, Henry, and Richard Blackaby. *Spiritual Leadership*. Nashville: Broadman & Holman, 2001. A fresh and challenging perspctive on leadership—which encourages all who lead to move from their own to God's agenda.

Briner, Robert A. *The Management Methods of Jesus*. Nashville: Thomas Nelson, 1996. Jesus, the manager? Bob Briner cites fifty-two ways Jesus' example teaches us superior business practices.

DePree, Max. *Leadership Is an Art*. New York: Doubleday, 1989. The former chairman of Herman Miller, Inc. offers practical gems of leadership in a short, highly readable (and memorable) format.

Guinness, Os. *The Call: Finding and Fulfilling the Central Purpose of Your Life*. Nashville: Word, 1998. Especially written for those who feel a deep longing to understand their unique life purpose—the ultimate "why" for living.

Overman, Christian. *Assumptions That Affect Our Lives*. Chatsworth, Calif.: Micah 6:8, 1996. The foundations of Western thought are traced back to two opposing traditions: the ancient Greeks, who fathered secular, human-centered rationalism, and the ancient Hebrews, who carried forward God's revelation. The legacy of these views profoundly affect our approach to business and occupations today.

Peabody, Larry. *Secular Work Is Full-Time Service*. Ft. Washington, Penn.: Christian Literature Crusade, 1974. Drawing primarily from the example of Daniel in the Old Testament, Peabody's book proves that there is no scriptural authority for the belief that serving God in business is any less spiritual than serving God in full-time ministry.

Pollard, C. William. *The Soul of the Firm*. Grand Rapids, Mich.: Zondervan, 1996. An inside look at Servicemaster through the eyes of its CEO reveals a vital emphasis on the individual worth of the firm's 200,000 employees.

Rush, Myron. *Management: A Biblical Approach*. Wheaton, Ill.: Victor, 1983. Rush, a consultant and management trainer, provides biblically based help on a variety of key management issues.